MESSAGING
MAGIC

*How to Confidently Convert Conversations to Cash,
Checks, and Credit Cards!*

Andrieka J. Austin

Visit www.thebossof.me/mmaudio to get your FREE gift to help you take the next step in adding more MAGIC to your message using the FREE audio/video resources that go along with this book!

"There is someone somewhere waiting on you to share your story, so they can share theirs. When you impact one life, you impact generations. It's when you let your light shine, you give others permission to do the same."

P.s. – Tell your story. People are waiting.

Friend, Fan, and Follow on Facebook and Instagram
@messagingmagic

Visit www.thebossof.me/mmaudio to get your FREE gift to help you take the next step in adding more MAGIC to your message using the FREE audio/video resources that go along with this book!

MESSAGING MAGIC

How to Confidently Convert Conversations to Cash, Checks, and Credit Cards!

content errors. Therefore, this book should serve only as a general guide and not as the ultimate source of subject information. This book contains information that might be dated and is intended only to educate and entertain. The Author and Publisher shall have no liability or responsibility to any person or entity regarding any loss or damage incurred or alleged to have incurred directly or indirectly by the information contained in this book. You hereby agree to be bound by this disclaimer. By reading this document, the reader agrees that under no circumstances are we responsible for any losses, direct or indirect which are incurred as a result of use of the information contained within this document, including – but not limited to errors, omissions, or inaccuracies.

Journey Girl Publishing 6472 Church Street, Suite 237 Douglasville, GA 30134 | (770)744-4475

Cover Photos: G-14 Studios, Atlanta, GA | Makeup: Sean "B. Breezy" Mac

Business; Small Business; Entrepreneurship; Women Small Business Owners; Women Entrepreneurs; Coaching; Business Coaching; Marketing; Communication; Messaging; Story-telling; Sales; Story-selling;

For more information about Andrieka "AJ" Austin or to book her for your event email aj@thebossof.me

OTHER WORKS BY ANDRIEKA J. AUSTIN

Click on the title or visit www.thebossof.me/books

Secrets of a Socialprenista; The Top 8 Mistakes Women Entrepreneurs Make That Keep Them Broke, Stuck, and Struggling in Their Business

#SpeakUp; 22 Ways to Go from FREE to Fee-Based Speaking

How to Be The Boss Of Me; 120 Questions to Ask Yourself Before You Launch Your Business

20 Reasons NOT to Start A Non-Profit Organization; and How to Still Make A Difference

The Journey Girl Guide to Teen Girl Self-Empowerment; Girl-friendly Tips, Tools, and Tidbits

Ariel Rising [Contributing Author]

Just Me!; Branding for Women in Business [Contributing Author]

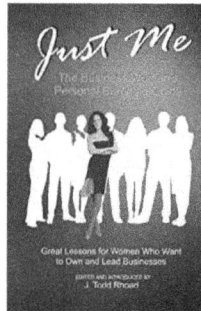

Coming Soon…

#WriteNow; How to Write Your First (or Next) Book in 24 Hours or Less!

LIVE EVENTS + SEMINARS HOSTED BY ANDRIEKA J. AUSTIN

Get Messaging MAGIC Mentoring at bit.ly/ineedmagic

#WriteNow [The Masterclass] at www.thebossof.me/writenowmini

#WriteNow [The Audio Course] – www.thebossof.me/write

#WriteNow [Writer's Intensive] – bit.ly/writenowretreat

SOCIAL MEDIA

Instagram: www.instagram.com/messagingmagic

LinkedIn: www.linkedin.com/in/messagingmagic

Facebook: www.facebook.com/messagingmagic

Twitter: www.twitter.com/messagingmagic

YouTube: bit.ly/bossofmetv

Visit www.thebossof.me/mmaudio to get your FREE gift to help you take the next step in adding more MAGIC to your message using the FREE audio that goes along with this book!

CONTENT

DEDICATION

This book is dedicated…

In loving memory of my mom, Daphne C. Minor, September 16, 1960 – April 14, 2008. You are the inspiration and reason I write. I love you forever.

To my brothers, Andraus "Dre Gutta" Austin and Kirsey D. Minor-Hart, you both are my favorite!

To Kayne, Jontae, Kelis, Noah, and my future nieces and nephews, this one is for you! #legacy

To Plezie Small, THANK YOU for your continued support – and for not letting me take the year off! You and my snack buddy, Chelsea, are the B.O.M. Glad to call you my Sister-in-Christ.

To Minister Veronica L. Limes, thank you for being. I appreciate your wise council and your support in my endeavors. I am grateful for you.

To Etoyi L. Billings thank you for your many years of prayer and support. It's an honor to call you one of my favorite friends and Sisters-in-Christ. I love you, Cletus!

To Dr. Greg and Angela Towler, and my Crossroads Church family, Boss of Me Small Group, volunteer/serving team, and Directors/Coaches - thank you for giving me a place and space to serve. Justin Owens, Keisha Tabbs-Barnes, Michelle Pethel, Brent Hardegree, and Joel

www.thebossof.me/mmaudio

Woods – Thank you for making me feel at home and for your continuous encouragement to share my gift with those who need it in the Kingdom of God.

To the #BomSquad, you ladies are all my business besties and the reason behind my MAGIC! You are the true meaning of being, 'The Boss of Me' [aka, "The B.O.M"}.

To Saving Our Children and Families [SOCAF] for honoring me for excellence and economic empowerment for girls and women around the world. You sparked my messaging journey. Thank you.

To Mrs. Vivian Lyons, thank you for your continued support throughout this book writing journey, allowing me to "sprinkle a little of my magic", and for constantly pouring love and light into this girl from the 'Honey Hole'. I appreciate you.

To the groups and organizations who made my first $100,000 for sharing my story possible, this all is because of you. Thank you!

CLIENTS

Who better to speak on 'Messaging MAGIC' than my own Business Besties (aka, 'The #BOMSquad') who have experienced it first-hand?...

Here's what a few of them had to say:

"I knew I needed help and I wanted to work with AJ. Before working with AJ, I had just been laid off from my job and I was trying to determine how to get started as a Life Coach. As a result of going through her program, I became a Coach and completed my first book! AJ has been so helpful and instrumental. She was the motivation I needed. Her process is set up to help you uncover your answers step-by-step."

- LaQuellis "Pixie Lee" McGee, Author

"Anyone looking to sign up for AJ's programs – whether it's getting help writing your first book, making your 'mess' your message, or increasing your income to make your first (or next) $25,000 building your coaching business; I highly recommend it."

- T. Renee Smith, Life Strategist

"I was not running an official business. I was just winging it. Working with AJ provided me much needed clarity, strategy, and focus. As a result, I hit my income goal in just a few short days! You will learn from one of the best. AJ is truly like a business best friend; comforting, knowledgeable, and supportive."

- Janae Martin, Life Purpose Coach

"I felt held back and ready to shut down. I was full of ideas and confusion. After hiring AJ as my Coach, I now have unwavering confidence. I needed to be coached by someone who is living the life I desire to live. AJ is anointed and authentic in her gift to deliver Christ-led material. If you are ready to be pushed into God's next step for your life, AJ is your personal Guardian Angel. She is the B.O.M!"

- Lakell Maxwell, Journey Guide

"My biggest challenge was scaling my business to profits. AJ's program helped me move through the blocks and fears I had. If you're looking for process and "aha moments", this program is for you. Thanks for an AWESOME journey, AJ!"

- Melia Houston, Tantric 360

FOREWORD

I have known Andrieka J. Austin ("AJ") since she enrolled in and successfully completed my Personal Life Coach Certification course in 2013. She was immersed in the knowledge and our company mission to *"Help people think better"*.

We both knew she was destined to be a trailblazer in the coaching community.

It is an honor to be her first Life Coach and Business Mentor. I have watched her dedication to make an impact with her work within the coaching industry expand along with her skills to help create positive change in the world.

She uses her real-world personal and professional experiences to effectively share her story of the 'struggle-to-success'.

She is a valued part of the Fast Coach Training team where she serves as Master Business Coach, Lead Trainer and Professional Speaker in our 1-day Personal Life Coach Certification immersive trainings – where she helps newly certified Personal Life Coaches by providing helpful tips and tidbits on how to become Coaches and grow their coaching business and brand.

She is a savvy entrepreneur and a talented "10" on our scale.

- Dr. Michael J. Duckett
Founder, www.fastcoachtraining.com

Dear Reader,

I want to share with you what I recently read in the book, *The Black Woman Millionaire*, by Dr. Venus Opal Reese.

It really spoke to me.

Consider this my Love Letter to you!

"You are the answer to millions of people's prayers and your life has prepared you for such times as these. Let your light shine so brightly that the millions of people for whom you are the answer to their prayers can find you – and pay you top dollar! Millions of people are waiting to be inspired by your work. LET THE WORLD HEAR YOU. Be the answer to millions of people's prayers. Let yourself be used for something bigger than you!"

- Dr. Venus Opal Reese
Black Woman Millionaire

YOU'RE ONE
CONVERSATION AWAY...

---

ow to Win Clients Without Feeling Stressed Out About Marketing Your Business – should've been the name (or at least the subtitle) of this book!

But, it's not.

You see, there's this little-known thing called 'Messaging MAGIC' (Hence, the actual title of this book!).

Hardly anyone is talking about it.

But when you learn it and use it, it can make all the difference in how fast people buy from or sign up to work with or do business with you.

It could make or break your failure or your success in your business.

And to think, you're only one conversation away…

It's for women entrepreneurs who are trying to get more customers or clients (people to buy from you, support you, learn more about what you do, and refer other business to you).

It's all about how to stop blending in and start standing out in your industry by telling your story (marketing your message) in an

1

authentic way that goes beyond titles, taglines, and bios – in a way that confidently converts conversations to clients, cash, checks, and credit cards.

It's your key to how to stop feeling like you're begging people to buy from you, and how you can still make money using this little-known trick that almost instantly puts your marketing on cruise control without you feeling overwhelmed (or like you don't want to bother or annoy people).

'Messaging MAGIC' is the key to marketing your business, winning over more customers and clients, having more people support what you do and tell others about you plus refer you out to their friends, family, fans and followers after they hire you (which instantly increases your impact, influence, and income) – and this is only obtainable through what you're about to read in the upcoming pages.

What is 'Messaging MAGIC', you ask? It's kind of like having your own little personal team of fairies flying around with their magic wands sprinkling golden magic dust on every word you say when you tell people about your business – instantly makes people want to buy from you, support you, and tell others about how great you are and how powerful your message is!

You may be thinking, *"I don't want to tell my business. I was taught not to 'talk outside the house' and to keep my personal business to myself."*
You may be thinking, *"No one wants to hear my story because it's boring, uninteresting, will take up too much time or is too long to tell".*

You may be thinking, *"I don't want to put my client's (or anyone from my past's) business 'out there'".*

You may be thinking, *"It doesn't take all that. Do I really need to tell my business and show how I struggled just to get someone to buy from me or support what I do?"*.

You may be thinking, *"I'm not good at telling jokes and I'm a bad storyteller"*.

You may be thinking, *"I'm just getting started and I don't have any client stories yet and mine are not that interesting"*.

If any of these statements ring true for you and you feel that you or your client's stories won't be interesting enough to compel someone to buy from you, read on.

If you don't want to offend, 'step on toes' or 'put anyone's business 'out there' – including your own – trying to convince people to buy from or sign up to work with you, read on.

If you're not sure if or how much adding stories (aka, 'sprinkling MAGIC' on your message) will increase your sales, read on.

If you feel like someone might get mad at you for telling too much of your story, I'll shared with you how to put your business 'out there' without putting your business (or anyone else's business) "out there".

People love to hear the stories behind a business brand and what makes you so passionate about what you do and w*hy* you do it.

I created 'Messaging MAGIC' because I'm tired of hearing people try to explain what they do, but not *why* they do what they do and the impact it has on changing lives.

They also leave out the experience and the results on what it's like to potentially do business with them.

They also fail to answer the question, *"Why should anyone care about what I do?"*.

Let's discuss this for a moment.

Whether you're introducing yourself to one person at a networking event or a few hundred people as you're speaking on a stage, it's necessary for you to learn how to relate what you do and *why* you do what you do in your business, using the power of your story.

My goal for this book is to show you how.

AUTHOR'S NOTE

I recently learned that 95% of the books on the shelves at Barnes and Noble never sell more than 1,000 copies (Dean Graziosi).

Thank you for helping us beat those odds by purchasing your copy of this book!

I'm AJ, aka "The Messenger"; Master Business Coach, Professional Story-teller and Host of empowering conversations.

You know the conversations that get so good and the stories that get so sweet you just want to package them up and turn them into Amazon best-sellers, like the one you're reading now?!

You know the conversations with parts of your story that are so juicy you want to travel the globe and share it through speaking to as many people as you can?

When you take your story and turn it into a book, then use your book to create a product or program, and share your love for telling your story with anyone who will listen, you are packaged for what I call, 'Passive Profits' – to help you instantly increase your impact, influence, and income.

This book is my example of how I did just that.

I currently create my own schedule, receive a passive income, and work from wherever, whenever (I'm currently sitting in a virtual, on-demand co-workspace typing this out to you) – I did the edits to this book around 3:00am est sitting behind my desk at my business office headquarters, just a few miles west of downtown Atlanta, GA, and the final, final edits at several Starbucks locations and beautiful coffee shop patios with a view!

Anywho,

I travel (sometimes), speak virtually and at live events where I train women entrepreneurs just like you on how you can make having a business work for you too.

My motto is, *"I do what I love and I LOVE what I do."*

But it has not always been this way.

It took me fifteen years to graduate college.

I have had more than one corporate position "dissolve". One resulted in me becoming homeless – sleeping in my car, and on the floors and couches of family and friends.

In addition to this, I remember the day my mom died.
It was on the same day my divorce from a five-year marriage was finalized.

I share more about my journey through it all in the upcoming pages and how God has allowed me to go from homelessness to becoming a homeowner with rental property, lease my first office space to headquarter my businesses, and so much more.

This book is based on and inspired by my journey from the struggle to success in entrepreneurship as a Christian woman in business to growing a globally impactful coaching enterprise, plus how I use what I'm going to teach you to get paid to get paid.

You will read my story of some of the hardest things I've been through and overcame successfully in my business and how you too can make your "mess" your money-making marketing message in your business or professional organization and association.

I promise to share insight into my journey to help you build and boost your confidence as a woman in business and help you affirm your purpose within your business by sharing who you are and *why* you do what you do in your business (that's the 'Messaging MAGIC' secret).

You'll also get to hear about other women entrepreneurs who (just like you) needed my help and support sharing their story too.

This book is your chance to learn how you can profit from your "mistakes" (like I currently do) and learn something from the experiences of someone who's 'been there'.

Let me let you in on something I haven't shared with many people outside of my inner circle of spiritual leaders. I openly operate in the gifting and the anointing of the prophetic. I have been prophetically activated and challenged to move to a higher realm of prophetic discernment in all that I do with my clients within my coaching business, in my books, and when I speak.

In this book, I share with you what I hear (and have heard) from God with more faith, clarity, and confidence than I ever have in my previous writings (see the "Other Works by Andrieka J. Austin" section a few pages back).

I have a Word. I see and hear *your* message clearly.

As 'The Messenger', I speak the truth in love. This authority is what makes me different than any other Coach.

I am here to wake up the MAGIC in you, and help you push further into your purpose – using the power of your story.

ON ANOTHER NOTE...

Whether you're a mom, an aunt (like me!), a grandmother, or you have a significant female presence in someone's life – if you're reading this book, you may be one of the women entrepreneurs or small business owners who are not meeting your sales goals and/or you're consistently falling at or below the low-income level in your small business.

You may even feel a bit embarrassed when people ask you how your business is going.

Those you love may look at you and wonder, *"Does entrepreneurship even work?"* or, *"Is she really making money?"* or, *"Why doesn't she go get a real job?"*.

These questions may even linger in your mind.

I know what that's like.

In the early stages of my business, one of my friends would email me job openings to let me know who was hiring.

Embarrassing.

If you're a woman legacy builder who is building her business for your children, grandchildren, and the next generation, you may not be leaving the type of legacy you initially set out to leave.

This problem is costing you the clients you could be reaching, the admiration of your children, the respect of your friends (see example above) and those you love.

It's also costing the women who are looking to you as their woman small business owner role model to wonder what they can do to be more like you (or not).

Think of all the change you could be making, but you're not – because you're consistently performing the same routines that are not getting you or your business the results you know you need.

Imagine if you knew what to do to finally get exactly where you want to be in your business.

You'd probably be proud to no longer be a statistic (more on that later).

Well, no worries.

You'll soon be on a path to becoming a woman entrepreneur with a working, money-making system that allows you to bring in the money you need in a way your family will be proud to carry on.

CAN YOU IMAGINE...?

S ee yourself receiving invitations to travel and speak around the world and touching lives by sharing your story.

Just imagine people asking you, *"How did you do it? How did you go from struggling to success in your business?"*.

You'll be the woman small business owner who will potentially stand in front of thousands of other women small business owners who ask you interview questions like:

- *"What tip(s) or piece of advice or guidance can you share with us to help us get to where you are now?"*
- *"What's the secret formula that got you here?"*
- *"Who helped you get here?"*
- *"When did you realize you'd reached your limit, pushed yourself far enough, knew you had enough, had done everything you knew to do, and that it was time to reach out to get help with growing your business?"*
- *"What did getting help in your business look like for you and how much did it cost you?"*
- *"What did you sacrifice to get to where you are today?"*
- *"How can I be more like you?"*

I am often asked these questions and told the following:

- *"We sat in and graduated from the same class. We even started our journey together. How are you so far along in your business?"*
- *"You're a trailblazer and a role model. I look up to you."*
- *"What's your secret? Can you help me?"*
- *"I've been following your journey and witnessing your growth."*
- *"Thanks for traveling to come speak to us."*

If you do what I show you how to do in this book (and don't skip a step), you too will be known as an influencer with massive impact around the world.

You'll smile every time you look at your income statement knowing you've superseded your revenue goals.

You'll be *that* woman small business owner.

You'll officially be the #legacybuilder you desire to be.

Even when you are no longer here in earth, your presence will still be felt because of the knowledge you shared and the example you set for those who come after you.
Your children will call you blessed.

Your friends will be proud to know you (and share about what you do to others).

Your family will speak highly of you.

People will show up at your events and buy your products, hire your services, and tell their friends about you too.

Your ideal future clients will open every email from you, reply to them, forward them to their friends who they know could also use your business products and services.

That's exactly what happened to (and for) me, once I started using 'Messaging MAGIC'.

Imagine knowing how to tell (and sell) your story using a blueprint for sharing a magical money-making marketing message.

If you're ready to stop blending in and start standing out in your industry in an authentic way that confidently converts conversations to clients, cash, checks, and credit cards, 'Messaging MAGIC' is for you!

This is your guide on how to tell your story – what to include, and what's okay to leave out (even if you are 'not ready' to share *that* part of your story yet).

Before we dive in, select which of the following statements you most closely relate with:

- **You know God has called you to do what you do in your business.**
- **You have a big mission and a great vision in your business.**
- **You want to "get out there" in a bigger way and help the people you serve on a much bigger level (but you're just not sure how).**
- **You know you want to share your story but you're "stuck".**

Whether you selected one or all-of-the-above, keep reading.

Before we dive in, head over to www.thebossof.me/mmaudio for your FREE gift from me that's jammed pack with a helpful resource for taking your message to the next level.

Yours in M A G I C,
Andrieka "AJ" Austin

P.s. – This book is best for you if you...

Are a woman small business owner or entrepreneur who's ready to stop feeling like you're begging people to do business with you. You're ready to stop blending in and start standing out, and you'd love for others to ask you what you do, sign up to do business with you, and tell others about you!

HERE'S THE THING

"Facts tell. Stories sell. Tell a great story and get prospects to buy."
- Russell Brunson

According to the United States Women's Chamber of Commerce, "70% of women small business owners make less than $25,000 a year".

This is what I call a startling statistic.

I believe this number will continue to get bigger because women small business owners and entrepreneurs are seeking opportunities outside of themselves to make more money in their business.

They are seeking government contracts, loans, venture capitalists, angel investors, sponsorships, scholarships, or someone to sow a financial seed to "support" their business. I've even received the last two.

However, waiting on these to come through only feed the aforementioned statistic and contributes to more of our world's poverty level.

This is not good.
Especially for those in business who say, *"I'm in business to leave a legacy for my children"*.
If you've ever said that, now is when you get one step closer on your journey to success.

Coming up, I'll share the key to unlocking what's next for you in your business.

I thank you for allowing me to be a part of your process.

In the words of my Pastor, Bishop William H. Murphy III, *"You have everything you need to succeed"*.

That includes this book.

I am sure you agree with me that it's time for your next level of success.

I've known since I was six years old that I have been called to do great things.

Chances are, you are reading this book because for a long time, you too have known that there is something greater within you.

You've been called and chosen for such a time as this.

Today is the day you start (or continue) the journey.

You can't leave a legacy on less than twenty-five thousand dollars a year in revenue.

I am here to encourage you to keep pressing forward.

I want to help you choose to be more and do more in your business.

Helping women entrepreneurs get their God-given vision and ideas out of their heads, onto paper, and into action (and make more money) is my passion.

Teaching an entrepreneur how to use what she knows and leverage her expertise to instantly increase the impact, influence, and income in her business is what I do.

Whether you're in the startup phase of your business and trying to get things off the ground, the sustainability phase and trying to keep things up and running, or in the scaling mode, implementing systems that will make things work more with less of you in your business – you will learn from what I share about my journey and what it takes to work through the 'struggle-to-success' process.

I pledge to be your transparent, blunt, tell-it-like-it-is, no excuses, tough-love-giving, down-to-earth business best girlfriend, as I show you what it took for me to go from struggling and living out of my car, to living out my own personally defined definition of the word, *'success'*.

Also, let's connect over at www.thebossof.me/mmaudio where you'll receive your FREE gift of additional resources to go along with this book when you join the community and raise your hand to receive ongoing support from me on your journey.

If you are at a place where you just need someone to believe in (and with) you, I recommend you continue reading this book – and take my advice to join my community using the links I've shared above, below, on the previous and following pages – and take me up on the transformational invitation at the end of this book!

WHY?

"When you let your light shine you give others
permission to do the same."
- Marianne Williamson

A few years ago, someone asked me why I do this.
It was YouTube Sensation and Life Coach, Marie Forleo.

Her exact question was, *"AJ, what's your why?"*

From this conversation, I concluded that my "why" comes from the U.S. Women's Chamber of Commerce statistic I shared with you a few pages back.

According to some state income guidelines, earning only twenty-five thousand dollars a year in revenue from a single income source (usually a business) is considered poverty level, especially if you're trying to financially support a family.

I spent most of my childhood living a low-income lifestyle.

It doesn't feel good to be broke.

Especially when you're an adult working for yourself and you have the 'ability to create your own wealth' (See Deuteronomy 8:18 in The Holy Bible).

After reading, researching, and investing in myself, I realized that poverty is a mindset.

So, I shifted mine.

Then, I decided to focus on educating, empowering, and encouraging other women entrepreneurs on how to become self-empowered.

I believe that if women hold eighty percent of the buying power in today's economy, imagine what would happen if we did business together.

Together, we would exceed the income glass ceiling and provide support for ourselves, our families, and each other.

So, thank you for investing in me and other women business owners through purchasing your copy of this book.

As a Master Business Coach and a Professional Storyteller, I show women entrepreneurs and small business owners how to successfully get from where they are to where they want to be in their business by sharing my own personal story of the struggle to my success.

I also share the ins-and-outs of the day-to-day operations with a few female interns I mentor from local universities here in Atlanta and abroad – helping them fulfill their dream of becoming a successful woman in business.

That's my why.

That's why I am in business.

That's why you're still reading this book.

I know what it's like to have a head full of ideas but no one to share them with who can point you in the right direction and share valuable resources to help you create a money-making masterplan and hold you accountable throughout the process.

I understand that there are thousands of women small business owners around the world who need help with all-of-the-above to take their business to the next level and get their message out into the world.

MOVING ON

Now back to why you're reading this book.

If you're like the women I often meet and coach who say, *"AJ, I'm building a legacy for my family"*, I want to ask you, "How?".

As your Coach (throughout the time it takes you to read this book – and maybe beyond!), I must be honest with you.

I told you I'd be straightforward with you.

If your business' yearly revenue receipts fall under the twenty-five thousand dollar per year mark, you are not building a legacy.

It's time o-u-t for being a poverty-minded, low-income business owner.

This may be hard to hear.

But it's true.

As a woman, you're part of a minority of the genders within our population.

As a woman small business owner or entrepreneur, you're a minority of a minority.

If you're a woman small business owner or entrepreneur within an underserved group of people, you're a minority of a minority of a minority and the likelihood of you falling within the aforementioned statistic increases drastically.

Women small business owners will continue to be a part of this growing problem of not making enough money in their business until we realize the power that our own story holds – and how it directly influences the amount of money we make in our businesses.

Majority of women small business owners and entrepreneurs may never consider their story when it comes to making more money in their business.

Before picking up this book, you may have been one of them.

Why?

It's because maybe you're sharing with people *what* you do, but not *why* you do what you do in your business.

Maybe you've been trying to get results and you're wondering, *"What am I doing wrong?"* or *"What do I need to tweak?"*.

Maybe you feel like you're doing everything you know how to do, but nothing's working and you're ready to give up on this small business ownership or entrepreneurship thing.

Maybe you resonate with the following:

No matter what you do, people:
1. Register for, but don't attend your events
2. Don't show up on your conference calls
3. Don't reply to your repeat "follow-up" emails

4. Don't comment on your social media pictures, posts, and videos you tag them in about your business
5. Read, but don't respond to your numerous inbox messages

Think about what will happen to the legacy you want to leave through your business legacy if you don't correct this.

The truth is, you may be out of business soon.

'Messaging MAGIC' to the rescue!

Once you practice 'Messaging MAGIC' (keep reading, I'll share what that is soon), you'll no longer have to tag people in your social media posts or spam their inboxes hoping to get their attention, trying to get them to "support", buy from, or do business with you.

Your fans will soon begin to happily share about your business on their own social media pages – often without you asking.

People will want to bring their friends, fans, and followers along the journey of supporting, showing up for, and doing business with you.

You'll host conference calls that get people to show up and bring others along who you can help with your business products and services as well.

People will talk about you (in a good way) – even when you're not in the room.

This is positive.

This is profitable.

This is where your passion and your purpose come into play, all because you took the time to acknowledge you needed help to get you from where you are now to exactly where you want to be in the near future.

You started this journey knowing you're not alone.

I pray you find peace in knowing that there are millions of women across the world who are right where you are in this moment.

Coming up, I'll share more of my story to show you how I discovered what took me from the poverty level in life and business to becoming the successful woman I just described to you who consistently receives calls, emails, and inbox messages, and referrals from people saying, *"We just want to be in your presence. Can you attend our event to speak and/or give us your professional feedback? Or, can we attend an event you're hosting? We'll gladly compensate you for your time."*

I'm the woman serving behind-the-scenes with well-known celebrities in the coaching industry who charge multiple tens-of-thousands of dollars just to sit at the same table with them – I've already name dropped a few here earlier, and I'll share more in the upcoming pages (also see photos - and proof - on www.thebossof.me).

They know my name, my story, and my skills – all thanks to 'Messaging MAGIC'.

My gifts have made room for me (see Proverbs 18:16 in The Holy Bible) and yours will too.

I hope you're ready to embark on this new journey with me.

I must let you know that it's not easy.

It takes a lot of hard work, focus, and determination to do the work and get it 'out there'.

But, I believe you're willing.

There are thousands waiting and wanting to hear your story and I believe you're ready to tell it.

Right?

The issue of not making more money in your business is solvable.

On your journey to the solution, pay close attention to the 'Activity' boxes throughout the rest of the reading to help you get to your answers faster.

Get your personal journal ready and I'll see you in the next section.

MESSAGING M A G I C

"But remember the Lord your God, for it is he who gives you the ability to produce wealth, and so confirms his covenant, which he swore to your ancestors, as it is today."
- Deuteronomy 8:18

Messaging MAGIC is a five-part formula I share with women around the world to help them take their business (and their message) from poverty to prosperity.

It's a step-by-step formula I'll share with you during our time together.

M-A-G-I-C is actually an acronym.

It means something (hence, the all caps on the letters in the word, *"MAGIC"*).

Here's the breakdown of this term:

<u>**M**</u> is for **'Market'**, which is where you tell your people about the results they want or wish for and how you're the business person to help them by

- Sharing parts of your business journey story about where you've been (and how it relates to them)
- Pointing to successes (yours and your past and present clients)

- Giving a glimpse into the "this could be yours!" thought process

A is for **'Align'**, which is means the message in story lines up with the outcome of what you're hoping for and proves the overall point/purpose of you sharing your story/message and it
- Matters to your people's outcome because it's what they want or wish for in their lives
- Shows a balance of where they are now compared to where they could be
- Connects-the-dots to where they want to be and why working with you could potentially get them there faster

G is for **'Guide'**, which is where you hold their hand on and walk with them
- Through a quick summary/snapshot of your progressive journey (even if you're still on it)

I is for **'Inspire'**, which is where your story and your message uplifts their spirits and leaves them there in a way that's
- Upbeat, positive, seeing themselves in you and believing that *"this could be me too!"*

C is for **'Convert'**, which gets people to raise their hands to get what they want or wish for…from you, by
- Calling you
- Emailing you
- Registering for your next event
- Buying your product
- Hiring your services
- Joining your email list
- Inboxing you on social media

- Supporting to your cause (i.e., becoming a member, signing up to be a sponsor, making a donation, etc.)

Learning and using the five-point 'Messaging MAGIC' formula offers great results for:

1. Your website's 'About Us' page
2. Your introductory talk or speech
3. The opening chapter, introduction, or preface to your new book

> **Need help writing a book?** Check out
> bit.ly/2019writer

4. Your answer to, *"So, (insert your name here), what do you do?"* – at a networking event
5. Bringing you in (and connecting with) your next customer or client
6. Your answer for how to uniquely stand out in your industry
7. Getting people to beg to work and/or do business with you
8. Receiving unlimited business referrals
9. Selling multiple orders and copies of your new book
10. Getting booked to speak more
11. Hearing about how others 'talk about you' when you're in (and out of) the room
12. Sharing the mission, vision, and story of your professional organization or association

In the upcoming sessions, I'll share with you the simple secret for how to engage in a conversation and apply the 'Messaging MAGIC' formula.

Allow me to show you the way.

Diving into all five steps in MAGIC will help your message **M**arket, **A**lign, **G**uide, **I**nspire, and **C**onvert conversations into clients, cash, checks, credit cards, and contracts.

Sound good?

Awesome.

Here's how we'll do it:

<u>STEP 1</u>

In the first step, we begin the process of identifying the power that sharing your story can have in your business.

We walk through your story of what got you "here".

ACTIVITY:

1. **How did you end up where you currently are in your business?**

2. **What was the process of evolving from the little girl who once-upon-a-time had a dream, and may have even known she wanted to someday be in business for herself?**

3. **How did she become the woman who now has others looking up to her?**

4. **Do you recall the "struggle" (or at least parts of it) that got you to where you are today in your business?**

Think about it.

Start there.

Write it down.

Take a moment to think through what you've been through.

We'll call this your 'Struggle-to-Success Story'.

Your struggle doesn't have to be involved in violence, being in a hostile situation, or the drastically life-altering trauma of homelessness, like mine is.

You can define the term *"struggle"* in your own way.

It's simply the point of your story where obstacles first appeared – leading to how to overcome them.

In this section, I advise you to only tell the parts that DO NOT include what I call, "The 3 C's".

If any of the following three things below describe your response to some parts of your 'struggle/start up' story, simply leave it out.

You're not ready to tell *"that part"* of your story if you are still:
  1. Cursing about *"that part"* of your story
  2. Crying about *"that part"* of your story
  3. Calling someone 'out of their name (also known as "cussing") about *"that part"* of your story

Again, even one of the "3 C's" means that you're probably not ready to share *"that part"* of your story, and it's okay.

Move on.

However, if you've been through an obstacle that you were able to turn into an opportunity and it played a part in leading you to where you are today – hopefully you're now in a good, safe, and positive place - share your that part of your story and reach others with it if you so choose.

Think back to what got you here.

Reading this book, searching for a new way to reach more people, make more money, and grow your business.

Here's a snapshot of what's to come:

Coming up, I'll show you how I went from struggle to success in my current business and I'll fill you in on what I call "the dirty details" of *"that part"* of my story so you can see how it's done.

I'll share with you how my journey led me to be right here with you, writing this book and successfully speaking and coaching women just like you through the story-sharing and book writing process.

Will you be one of the next success stories?

MY STORY

"You must persuade people to believe in what you are doing, and
you do that by mastering the art of story-telling."
- Russell Brunson

I t was April 14, 2008.

I had scheduled time off work from a corporate nine-to-five job I landed through a staffing agency, thanks to a referral from a new friend visiting the States from London.

That day, I went down to my local courthouse for the hearing that would make my divorce from a five-year marriage final.

I happily signed on the dotted line (you read that right!) and headed out of the courtroom.

I approached the elevators and pushed the "Down" button.

The elevator doors opened.

I stepped inside and pushed the button labeled "Lobby" as I thought to myself, *"I wonder how many people have been as happy as I am to exit this building right now?!"*.

I was excited about *"that part"* of my day (and my story) finally being over.

Because I was already off work that day and had some free time after the trial, I had also scheduled a television appearance with a local NBC Studios affiliate to promote a new business I started after work and on the weekends.

This would be my second time on television with this new business brand.

I was so excited.

Back at the elevator, I exhaled as the doors began to close and I saw my now ex-husband for the last time.

Then, my phone rang from inside my purse.

I answered it in a great mood feeling excited about what the rest of my day would hold for my future and the growth of my new business.

"Hello?", I answered.
On the other end was my cousin calling to tell me that my mom had just passed away.

Wow!

Talk about life-altering.

The same moment I was closing one chapter of my life, another was beginning to unfold.

I can't remember what I said or thought during that conversation but, a snapshot of one of the memories that comes to mind now is about how once I was finally outside of the courthouse building that day, stopped and stood in the middle of the road - wanting to scream aloud - but silently praying and asking God what He wanted me to do.

After the first call with the news of my mother's death, my phone rang consistently with calls from family members and other unknown numbers asking me, *"So, what are you going to do about your mother's house, and her funeral arrangements, and her nearly half-million dollars in medical expenses, and…?"*

I wanted to shout, *"This is the same conversations I'm having with God at the moment! Give me a minute, please!"*

I'm the eldest and only girl of my mother's three children, hence the numerous calls about my plans on how to handle this.

This meant that the responsibility of 'what to do next' all fell on my shoulders.

I was left picking up and putting together the pieces of my mom's life just as I had to do with my own previous life.

My mom was forty-seven years old.

She was also a fifteen-year small business owner.

Her biggest dream in life was to be a homeowner and have a brand-new house built from the ground up.

She did that.

After calling on a few of my friends to pray with me, I decided to go clean out her new home, handle her personal affairs, pay for her funeral arrangements, and settle her medical expenses.

One thing I didn't mention earlier is that during this time in my own personal life, I was living in a homeless shelter for women, then in a prison that had been converted into a transitional housing program for the working poor.

Before that, I was sleeping on the floors, couch pillows, pull-out-sofa beds, and (believe it or not) in the guest bedroom of the same house I was now responsible for cleaning my mother's belongings out of.

I was later offered the option to own my mother's home.

I accepted.

This was my life now.

From homeless to homeowner.

The story continues.

A few days later, I found myself back at work locked in a small bathroom stall crying uncontrollably.

Absenteeism was frowned upon at this job and I had already taken a day off for the divorce, then, my mom's funeral a few days later, and then my Aunt's funeral a week after that.

However, my Supervisor at the time recommended I take an additional day or two to get myself completely together.

I did.

While on bereavement, I received a phone call that my team and our entire department had been downsized while I was away and that I did not have a job to return to.

At this moment I should've been sad.

But, I was happy actually about the job and position downsizing!

Why?

I worked 7am-7pm six days a week.

I was mentally and physically exhausted which led to panic attacks, chest pains, anxiety, crying uncontrollably, anti-anxiety and anti-depressant medications.

I remember being balled up at the top of the stairs in my home not recognizing myself or my life.

I had to snap out of it.

I fought.

I fought for the dream I've had since early childhood to create my own dream job.

Now was my opportunity to live that dream.

This is what I've always wanted.

It was time to pursue my entrepreneurial dream.

This was the same dream job and position I used to wish for deep in my soul while I sat in my corporate cubicle.

So, I decided to get up – from that day on - and seize this time as my chance to be in the place of freedom finally working for myself and determining my own destiny.

Once the dust settled from the series of my life events, I took some time to sit with God and process my thoughts on everything that had recently occurred in my life; dropping out of school, homelessness, the divorce, the death of my mom, and the downsize of my job.

I needed to get my story straight.

Everything that I'd been through as a result of that one day made me stronger, wiser, and gave me a deeper insight into who I am.

I read business books, researched successful entrepreneurs.

I attended networking events to fellowship with women who were in business for themselves and living the lifestyle I wanted to live.

I was now a newly unemployed, aspiring entrepreneur.

I noticed women often gave me their business cards filled with titles and taglines - some resembling a mini-resume.

I never cared to ask for more detail about what they did specifically in their businesses.

I was the person who glanced at a business card, slid it in my pocket (or in the nearest trash bin) after I excused myself from the conversation.

This was all because I didn't know (or understand):
1. *What* they did in their business
2. *Why* they chose this type of business (or *where* their passion came from) and *why* I should care – (aka, "their story")
3. *How* (or *why*) I could connect with them to help me get to my next level in my life or business (Note: not a sales pitch)

I wanted to hear their stories of *what* got them "here", in business for themselves.

After all I'd just came through a series of obstacles I was ready to turn into an opportunity for entrepreneurship in my life.

At one event, one of the speakers showed the audience a shoe box filled with all the business cards he'd collected over time.

I thought, *"Who keeps that many business cards?"* and, *"Has he reached out and connected with each of these people?"*

I then used the contact information on the cards to gather the email addresses of a few hundred of the women I networked with in order to share something valuable with each of them.

Here's a snapshot of my email to them, *"Hi, my name is AJ. We recently met while networking. I'm new to the business community and I would love to know what your number one struggle is in your business".*

Surprising, huh?

Flow with me here.

I figured, maybe if I was having trouble understanding *why* they were in business (their story), maybe they were having trouble sharing it (or maybe they didn't know to share it) – and this is where they were stuck or struggling.

From the email conversations, I learned that there are around twenty universal business struggles that most women face in their business, all which resulted in not making much money in their business.

So, I wrote a book called, *Secrets of a Socialprenista.*

It features the top eight mistakes women in business told me they made that left them broke, stuck, and struggling in their business and I offer them inspiration for the journey of overcoming each of these.

Who knew this is where I would land?

I was now giving women insight on how to get unstuck, keep moving forward, and potentially make more money in their business.

This was now my new goal.

I already had business experience from running several businesses, along with the one I mentioned earlier (remember the one I was supposed to be on television promoting the day my mother passed away?).

From my own experience, I knew what it was like to be a woman in business needing to make more money, but having your peers looking up to you – thinking you were doing fine.

Writing this book gave me a new platform to share my story (remember the one I sat with God to put it all together?), along with a few secrets I uncovered from the hundreds of email and phone chats with women in business about why (and where) they were broke, stuck, and struggling in their business – plus, what to do about it.

The book you're reading now is what came next.
Once you discover and get a handle on the mistakes to avoid as a business owner (and how), you're ready for 'Messaging MAGIC'.

This is where you say what you do in your business, and *why* people should care - using the power of your story.

I've studied this process for years.

I've formulated the simple steps that most people don't know exist when sharing about who they are and what they do in their business.

If you're at a point in your business where you're ready to stop trying to figure this 'make more money' thing out on your own, I advise you implement the 'Messaging MAGIC' method in your marketing and sales process.

Implement what you've read so far (and what's to come) as you learn the process.

Trust the process.

Your message is within you.

Rehearse what you write out for yourself in your journal until it starts to flow naturally.

HOW I FIGURED IT OUT

"When you learn to tell stories well, you will increase your ability to persuade (sell) and attract (market)."
-Dean Graziosi

In 2014, I dreamt about making my first $100,000 as a Coach.

I successfully graduated the Coach certification and training course the year before with www.fastcoachtraining.com and their one-day intensive immersion process that quickly introduced me to the coaching industry and helped launch me into business.

I decided to sign up for my first online business coaching program with a Life Coach who modeled the success I desired.

This program was for entrepreneurs seeking to make their first or next one-hundred-thousand dollars in one hundred days.

I completed the program in two weeks.

First, I wrote out (by-hand) my hundred-thousand-dollar money-making marketing plan using what I learned in the program.

Then, I went back through all of my plan and typed it out.

It was then that I received a spiritual download and the revelation that I was now ready teach my plan as I implemented it in my business.

I knew there were other women who needed help drafting their game-changing money-making marketing maps too.

Next, I recorded a step-by-step audio course using my master plan.

I'm sharing a portion of that plan with you in the next few pages.

My plan, my message, my story, and lots of elbow grease has allowed me to replace the income I made in my past corporate positions with a large private non-profit university, Crisis Counselor for a women's domestic violence shelter, and an Enrollment Counselor for a government-funded agency (remember the one that downsized while I was out on bereavement?).

WHAT CAME NEXT...

I learned that when you share what you do in your business, it's all about the message you use to get people interested in doing business with you.

It's where the selling process begins.

However, it all starts before you even speak to them.

For instance, when someone:
- Googles your industry
- Visits your business Facebook, Instagram, Twitter, YouTube, or LinkedIn page
- Browses your website
- Joins your email list
- Reads your blog
- Sends you an email

- Calls your business phone and gets your voicemail

A conversation has begun before you have a chance to personally chat with them about who you are, what you do, and *why* you do what you do in your business.

With each of these steps, you've displayed what's known as your Signature Message/story and by the time someone has had the chance to go through each of these online channels, they know whether or not you're the right business person for them.

By the time they pick up the phone to call you, they're ready to continue the conversation you started online.

When the wording for *what* you do in your business, *who* do it for, and *why* you do it comes together with your personal story of *how* you got to where you are today as a leader in your industry, people will know you're the expert they need to do business with.

That's 'Messaging MAGIC'.

I've put together five magical points to help you not to have to figure this out on your own.

I've figured it all out for you.

It becomes clearer when you have a step-by-step formula to follow that helps your message <u>m</u>arket, <u>a</u>lign, <u>g</u>uide, <u>i</u>nspire, and <u>c</u>onvert conversations to clients, cash, checks, and credit cards!

Whether you're speaking from stage or networking face-to-face, 'Messaging MAGIC' will work for you.

Soon you'll be able to share your story with emotion, excitement, and expectation with a listening audience – all in a systematic way that leads to sales, sponsorship, membership and donor dollars.

I'm in love with messaging!

I breathe stories and story-selling.

I really enjoy hearing business leaders tell their stories of how they've turned obstacles into opportunities.

That's why you and I are here together today.

MESSAGING MAGIC SUCCESS

I was invited to a networking event for one-hundred female entrepreneurs, hosted by Atlanta entrepreneur, Dr. Nicole Garner Scott of '100 Female Entrepreneurs'.

As I walked into the event, I was instructed to fill out a name badge with only my name and what I *did* in my business (not my title).

I thought, *"What an appropriate game for 'Messaging MAGIC!'"*.

I wrote on my name badge that I did "magic".

I received a few bewildered glances when people read my name badge as I worked my way through the crowd.

I'm pretty sure they were thinking, *"What does she mean she does "magic"?"*.

Just before the event started, I met and chatted briefly with a lady named Mel.

She shared with me that she was in the direct sales industry.

Within a few moments of our conversation, I had helped her reword her thirty-second elevator speech.

When she was given the opportunity to introduce herself to the ladies at the event, she said exactly what we rehearsed and she was amazed by the instant reaction of the crowd.

To thank me for her results, she bought me lunch.

Shortly following the event, she posted a testimonial on my Facebook page about how I helped her using this thing called, 'Messaging MAGIC', and that she highly recommended me and encouraged those who needed help with what to say about *what* you do in your business (and *why*) to reach out to and connect with me.

> **Melissa Jacobs** shared a **live video**.
> Nov 19, 2016 at 9:10 PM · 🌐
>
> I was at this event today and had an amazing time. If you need that elevator pitch contact **Andrieka J. Austin** she is amazing.

When it was my turn to share more about myself, my business (and what kind of "magic" I did with the crowd), my heart began to beat fast and my hand shook uncontrollably with nervousness and excitement.

This was the first time I shared my new MAGIC with a live listening audience and a few hundred of my friends, fans, and followers on Facebook Live – as this moment was being video recorded on my cell phone [you can see the video at www.thebossof.me/mmaudio].

This was the moment I officially stepped into my role as a 'Messaging Magician'.

Although clients had witnessed it before (I'll get to that story in just a moment of how the name, 'Messaging MAGIC' came about!), it all became a tangible, new reality once I spoke it aloud.

The story I shared with you at the beginning of this book – you know the one about the divorce and death of my mother, job downsizing, and past life dissolving before me?

I shared this same story with a crowd of complete strangers.

I began with, *"Hello everyone, I'm AJ Austin, and I do magic. 'Messaging MAGIC', that is!"*

I started to see a few smiles in the crowd.

I went into the short version of my personal story (**M**arket), tied it in with the message of my business (**A**lign), and shared how I got to where I am today (**G**uide), revealed the meaning of it all (**I**nspire), and invited them to share their business cards and how they could connect with me so we could set up a time to chat more after the event (**C**onvert).

See how the **MAGIC** formula works?

The good news is that they all became engulfed with my story, so I shared for a bit longer than the initial thirty-seconds I was given, and I watched the MAGIC unfold.

The audience reaction was relieving as I shared what I did in my business (and *why*) - not just my title or a tagline.

Immediately afterwards, I received applause, compliments, comments, coaching call requests, and several invitations to speak.

The response from many in the crowd was, *"Oh, my gosh. That was amazing! You're such a great Speaker. Your story is so powerful. You're a warrior. Can you come speak to my group of ladies who need to hear your story and learn how to tell their story too?!"*

Another popular response from several of the ladies there was, *"Can you help me tell my story? When can I get on your calendar to get your help? I would love to work with you!"*

As a result of me sharing my 'Messaging MAGIC', by the end of the event there was a line of ladies waiting to hand me their business cards and requesting my help with sprinkling a little MAGIC on their message too.

As a result of me sharing my story, the event Hostess purchased one of my books and requested I host a 'Messaging MAGIC' workshop in her new event space!

A local radio personality was also in attendance at the event that day and once she heard my story and my offer to connect beyond the event, she requested one of my business cards and consistently kept in touch to request a time for us to meet and potentially work together.

Each lady desired a piece of the 'Messaging MAGIC' formula.

They desired the experience of what their new message could be to help them confidently convert conversations to clients, cash, checks and credit cards in their business.

Whenever I'm asked for a success story about someone who's used 'Messaging MAGIC', what I've just shared with you is one of the 'tip of the iceberg' stories of success I share – mine, Mel's, and Renee's (you'll meet her soon).

The moment at the event when I witnessed 'Messaging MAGIC' in action for such a large group of ladies who needed (and wanted) to learn how to apply it in their business too, I saw – in action – proof that this method works.

When you show up and share your story, you'll connect with at least one person (maybe more) in your audience every time.

I'm excited to share with you what has worked (and continues to work) successfully for me and my clients using this formula.

Next, I'll share with you exactly how I discovered 'Messaging MAGIC'!

HOW I DISCOVERED MAGIC

A few years ago, my client Ren invited me to lunch to get help with the promotional language for her new book.

She wanted my input (and she was paying for it! – both lunch *and* my advice!).

During our meal we discussed certain parts of her story.

In a past life she had spent three years in prison, and she wanted to somehow include this information in her sales messaging.

During our meeting, I said, *"You need to paint more of a mental picture for your readers to help them understand your story and place themselves in your shoes. Instead of saying you 'spent three years in prison', how about converting that into the exact number of days you were forced to wear an orange jump suit with thick socks and flip flops."*

She looked at me and said, *"AJ, I love it! It's like you do messaging magic! You took my "mess" of a story and sprinkled a little "magic" on it then gave me back a memorable magical message that matches my mission in a way I can happily share with people and help include them in my story to help them relate to it. Thank you!"*

In that moment, my heart skipped a beat.

I instantly fell in love with the words, 'messaging magic'.

I screamed, *"That's it! That's exactly what I do!"*

I'm glad we were seated in a booth in the back of my favorite vegetarian restaurant at the time.

It was during this delicious meal when she and I decided that from that moment on, those were the words I would use to describe what I do for my clients.

This was (and still is) my "sweet spot".

Wow, what a revelation!

After years of sharing my services with clients who needed them, I am pleased to say that this was the moment that officially defined it all.

This moment sealed the deal for me regarding what I do for women in their businesses.

This moment combined with my experience of sharing my story at the women's networking event changed everything for me.
It especially changed how I introduce myself at events I'm invited to.

Here's what I say now when someone asks, *"So, AJ, what do you do?"*

I respond with something like,

"I help women small business owners who are struggling to make money in their business learn how to confidently convert

conversations to clients, cash, checks, and credit cards – using what they already know and leveraging their expertise to instantly increase their impact, influence, and income in their business."

They respond with something like, *"Tell me more".*

I share my story and how I help women make what they do in their business sound super-sexy and makes people want to know more about how they can do business together and share their business with their family, friends, fans, and followers – who refer others *before* the first transaction even takes place!

See how that works?

When you use 'Messaging MAGIC' to share who you are and what you do in your business (along with *why* you do what you do), those you share your story with will want to tell others about the experience of 'that one time' they heard you speak and share your story in a way that really moved them.

They'll say things like, *"You gotta hear her speak. Her story is so powerful!"*

That's 'Messaging MAGIC'.

It's what your future clients are seeking from you through the power of your story (just like the one I've shared with you from the introduction of this book).

When you uncover the words to help you 'get your story straight', it's magical.

This is when you never have to worry about competition, because your competitors don't have your story.

Your competitors can never tell their stories and move a crowd to take action like you can with your *MAGIC*.

When I learned how to create and follow the five steps I'm sharing with you (and a few other quick secrets I'll share too) in a conversation, I began to fill my calendar, my roster of clients has grown, program sales and book sales have increased, I accept more speaking engagements, travel more, and still receive professional training opportunities and awards in my industry.

I am an expert.
As soon as I implemented MAGIC in my business, my bank accounts started to grow too.

My last book helped my business generate over $15,000 in revenue.

These numbers continue to grow today.

The secret is to share your story.

But not just any old made up story that you put a spin on to make it sound good or to make you look good or have your past sound bad.

I recommend that you put together your own true story.

Also, don't share a story that you've heard someone else share.

Don't lie.

Be honest.

Be open.

Put yourself in a place that makes you the expert (and the hero) of your story.

People will admire you.

However, you can only do this if you have the right formula and put it to use step-by-step.

Use the formula I've laid out for you.

Follow each step, in order.

Complete each part.

You can't do one step and leave another step out and expect to see great results in your business.

Disclaimer: My results or those of my clients may not be your same results.

However, I'm believing in you and with you that your results will reflect in your consistency of using the MAGIC formula.

Follow the steps and do things right and you'll have the potential to soar from where you are now in growing your business to increasing the amount of money that's currently in your business bank account (and the money that's coming to you and your business) as you share your story too.

Get excited for what's to come as you apply 'Messaging MAGIC' and get closer to obtaining the success you've been seeking.

MESSAGING MAGIC, continued...

M essaging MAGIC helps you master your message in a way that's just right for you and your business. It's designed to help you tell (and sell) your story while leaving a legacy with your words.

It's like having a blueprint for how to share your marketing message in a way that helps you know what to say (and what to leave out).

This five-step formula shares top tips on what to say when you're selling you, and how to make sure you're sharing what you do with a community of the right people who need to hear what you have to say.

All of this buillds on the foundation of running a profitable business and creating a system of success that increases your impact (the transformation you provide), influence (attracts the right people), an income (money coming into your business).

Together, we're about to dive into the experience and results your customers and clients get when they work with or do business with you.

The following is your own step-by-step MAGIC guide for how to develop your money-making marketing message using the 'Messaging MAGIC' method.

In the upcoming sections, we'll talk about how to make your marketing messaging MAGIC by making sure it…

1. <u>M</u>arkets – tells the *right* people about who you are, what you do, and why you do it

2. <u>A</u>ligns – lines up with where you are today in your business

3. <u>G</u>uides – gives your potential customers/clients insight into what it could look like if they were "there" (where you currently are today) too

4. <u>I</u>nfluences – helps your people think and act/make decisions like you need them to

5. <u>C</u>onverts – turns your conversations into clients, cash, checks, and credit cards

We'll also talk about your struggle-to-success story (another way to <u>M</u>arket).

We'll go over your solution strategy (<u>**A**</u>lign).

We'll dive into selling with your story (<u>**G**</u>uide).

We wrap it all up with a strategy for systematic story-telling success (<u>**C**</u>onverts).

Either way you look at it, it's **M A G I C**!

The outcome of this process is to help you help the people considering buying from or doing business with you, listen to you and make better, faster decisions to spend their money with you.

If you tell (and sell) your 'struggle story' and solution, people will be sold on your system of success.

If you don't tell your story less people will know about you, care about your business, buy your products or services or donate to/support your movement.

Messaging MAGIC helps you finally stop begging people to buy from you and start winning customers and clients without feeling stressed out or overwhelmed about marketing and sharing about your business.

With the knowledge in the upcoming pages, you now have access to a tool that will help you map out your magical money-making marketing message step-by-step (like where to start your story and how to navigate through it with ease using the MAGIC formula).

You'll get help thinking through your story while focusing on the results you provide, testimonials and raving reviews from your customers and clients.

We'll wrap it all up with a BONUS session on how to price, package and profit from your story where we'll walk step-by-step through how to figure out what you should be charging for your current products and services while including that in your magical message for making more money.

This information exists because people (like you!) need help telling their story in a way that ties into what you do in your businesss.

Your story is the quickest way to find your '*why*' and the reason behind why you do what you do in your business.

You'll be in a better position of power by formulating a conversation that's guaranteed to have people with their business cards and credit cards in-hand, ready to do business with you.

Once you find the MAGIC in your message people will be waiting to buy your books, products, hire your services, and happily make a donation to/support your cause.

Don't have a book out yet?

Go to bit.ly/2019writer right now to sign up to receive the help you need to get your book out this year.

Coming up, we'll walk step-by-step through how you share your story in a way that makes you and your business money.

I was in business nearly a decade-in-a-half before I discovered the power of my story.

When people requested that I share more of my story, I had already convinced myself that no one wanted to hear "all that".

I said, *"Who wants to hear about me being homeless, divorced, my mom's death taking place just hours later? No one wants to hear all my "business" and I don't want to put "all of that" out there."*

This was also a time when I was struggling financially and bringing in only about $2,000 a year in my business.

I had to tirelessly work part-time jobs to help supplement my business income.

I often wondered to myself:

- *"Is it always going to be like this?"*
- *"When will things "pick up" in my business?"*
- *"Why are people not wanting to pay to work with me?"*
- *"Where is the money?"*
- *"Why am I receiving constant requests to 'volunteer' my time for "exposure"?*
- *"Where is the income people claim being an entrepreneur brings in?"*
- *"I'm doing everything I know to do but at the end of the year, only a few thousand dollars has passed through my bank account"*
- *"What should I be doing diferently?"*

I sat waiting.

No customers.

No clients.

The money was somehow not appearing in my business bank account like I expected.

The days I didn't share my magical message through the power of my personal story turned into months my business struggled to get off the ground.
Maybe you're there too.

Keep reading.

LET THE MAGIC BEGIN...

MESSAGING MAGIC: A SNAPSHOT

As we continue our magical journey together, I encourage you to keep moving forward and keep in mind those who are eagerly awaiting to hear your story.

'Messaging MAGIC' is about story-telling to help you win customers and clients, get people to buy from you, support you, learn more about what you do, and refer others to you.

Now let's get into the steps of exactly how you can turn your conversations into clients, cash, checks, and credit cards.

Step 1: [Market]:

In the first step, we'll cover your story of significance while adding in your professional proficiencies. I'll break down parts of my story as the perfect speech model for you. You'll learn helpful tips to help you develop and share your own story as it relates to your personal and professional story of the struggle to success.

Step 2: [Align]:

In step two, we'll cover the four components of a good story and I'll help you form your own new short story summary to share.

Step 3: [Guide]:

In the third step, we'll cover your story of experience. You'll develop a five-step signature system of success - kind of like this MAGIC one!

Step 4: [Influence]:

In the fourth step, we'll walk through how to get others engaged in your story through brevity. You'll lay out your client cycle and you'll go through the 'Messaging MAGIC' Story Think Tank.

Step 5: [Convert]:

In step five, we cover setting up and selling your five-step signature system in recap and you'll learn who your system will work for. You'll share what your new clients will be able to do (and get rid of), plus you'll see how your system helps and who your system has helped.

WHO NEEDS YOUR MAGIC?

I*t* helps to know what to say when you're sharing your message, who needs to hear it, and how you can make a difference with it.

Take a moment to think about the person(s) who most needs to engage with you and hear you share your story's main-point and sub point plus how everything turned out successful for you.

Consider the characteristics of your favorite type of client to work with and what his or her current frustration looks like (what they want or wish for) before he/she hears your story.

For example, before working through the 'Messaging MAGIC' method my soon-to-be client sits alone in her home-office scratching her head in concern, anxiously trying to figure out ways to make more money in her business with no luck.

"I can't do this alone", she says.

"I need help! But, who can I call? Where can I go? What should I do? Who can help me? I've tried everything I could on my own. Am I doing this stuff right? I need answers!"

She turns to Google for a quick search on *"How to get clients"* or *"How to make money in my business quickly"*.

Then, the journey begins.

Here are the typical 10 step process she (and many women entrepreneurs and small business owners like her) goes through to find me through my MAGIC message.

Watch how the conversation convert to a client with cash, a check, and/or a credit card!

Step 1: She sees a link to a blog post or article I've written or a video I've recorded addressing her concern on 'how to make money quickly in your business'.

Step 2: She clicks, reads, likes, and shares the information with her online tribe and community.

Step 3: Out of curiosity, she searches for more of what I have to offer and how I can potentially help her make more money in her business as she clicks and snoops around on the rest of my online written blogs and video posts and website.

Step 4: Her search leads her to a page where I share my story (the same one I've shared with you) and she hears my passion for *what* I do, *who* I do it for, *why* I do it, and *how* I do it using my business products, programs, and services for women in business who look and sound just like her.

Step 5: Her research continues as she clicks the button to join my email list to stay up-to-date with what I currently have going on in my business and what I'm doing (or where I'll be) next.

Step 6: She sees and clicks on the social media icons on my website to friend, fan, and follow me online.

Step 7: She sees a social media post about where I'll be speaking live in-person at an empowerment conference for women, or she sees me on a Facebook LIVE, Instagram LIVE or video posted on YouTube about something called, 'Messaging MAGIC' and how it helps women confidently convert conversations to clients, cash, checks, and credit cards.

Step 8: During my talk, she hears me mention my tenth best-selling book, *Messaging MAGIC* (the one you're reading today). She heads back to my website (or Amazon) and buys the digital, print, and/or audio version of the new book and she receives all of the great digital bonuses that come with it – like you will too at www.thebossof.me/mmaudio.

Step 9: Completely sold on my story and the solution I have to offer her, she then revisits my website and excitedly signs up for a coaching call with me or a member of my coaching squad, (also known as, 'The BOM Squad').

Step 10: Out of eagerness and excitement from what she's learned within the book (the same one you're reading now) hearing me speak on my struggle-to-success story with passion, combined with true confidence from our coaching call, she then enrolls in the 'Messaging MAGIC' masterclass, and the rest is HERstory!

That's the power of 'Messaging MAGIC'.

Now, take a moment to list in your journal the layout of your very own customer journey process.

What does that look like for you and him/her?

Write it out in your journal, step-by-step.

FINDING YOUR MAGIC

Think back to what brought you to where you currently are, doing what you do in your business.

When you learn how to tell your story of what you've been through (the struggle), and how you've successfully overcome that hurdle, struggle, or challenge (the solution) in a quick and succinct way that doesn't bore your listeners or bring up raw, negative emotions for you, you begin to leave a legacy with your words.

Sharing a story also makes it easy for others to help you spread the word and tell their friends, fans, and followers about you and the transformational work you do in your business.

It also allows you to be sure that the right people (those who need and want to hear your message/story) will hear it.

Now that you know what to say and you understand who needs to hear it, we'll soon discuss how you can make money from sharing your story.

Your future clients will pay you to tell them more about your workshops, books, speeches, training videos, coaching services and/or training programs, if that's the route you desire to take in your business.

These are all places where you'll consistently plug your messaging and constantly see the impact and influence it has on your income.

You'll want to invest time in creating, sharing, and applying your story to your marketing message.

This also makes it easier to connect with your community of clients so that when you find them (or vice versa) they're attracted to you because you're speaking each other's language.

We've discussed your struggle, what to say when you're selling the concept of you being seen as the expert in your business (and making more money) because of what you've been through on your life and/or business journey.

This is one of the juicier parts of taking your business to the next level (and it's so much fun to do).

Now that we know exactly the type of potential client that's perfect for hearing your story, you'll be able to focus in on what to say to draw those types of people to you and your business.

People are inspired by personal stories.

Much of the time what draws them in is hearing the transparency of what it took for you to get to where you are (despite the journey from where you were and what you've been through).

This will often move and motivate the right prospects to work with you.

They want to invest in your story and your step-by-step signature system of solution and success.

More specifically, how you went through and successfully came out of a particular problem, dealt with a certain situation, and turned an obstacle into an opportunity.

The journey of where your life has taken you (in a way that shows them how they can overcome too) has a lot to do with where you are right now in your business.

Your truth.

Your daily motivation in and for your business.

Sharing your story encourages engagement and support from people who are attracted to your business.

NEXT...

Next, we'll design what's called your 'Super Sexy Signature Story'.

It's a similar concept to an elevator speech, but sexier!

It's that brief moment when you get to share "who you are" and "what you do" with potential prospects you might like to do business with and vice versa.

There are four major components of your speech that can help convince a potential new client that you're just what they need.

Get your journal ready, turn the page, and let's dive in.

[MARKET]:

[MARKET]:
USING YOUR STORY OF
SIGNIFICANCE

L et's discuss your story.

This will soon be known as your 'Signature Story' or your 'Story of Significance'.

This is your moment.

Your truth (aka, your MAGIC message).

It's the truth, according to you.

When used right, it's also the way to magnify your business marketing message (and your money).

This story takes your potential clients on a journey of something you've experienced or been through at some point in your life that brought you to the point you're at now in your business.

The current business you're building is exactly what your clients and customers want to hear about as it relates to your story.

The point is to share how you turned your obstacles into an opportunity, your test into your testimony, and your struggles into your current success.

This is what will appeal to and attract your future customers and clients.

Your potential customers/clients want to know you've been where they currently are and that you understand their journey on a personal level, which allows you to have something in common with them – all the more reason they'll be drawn to doing business with you.

This starts to build their belief in you as you establish rapport and draw them in closer to becoming a customer or client.

This part of your story is not about your degrees or professional experience.

It's more of an opportunity to share who you are, from the inside out.

This is your time to share your message of how you have "been there" (where your potential customer or client currently is), and "done that" (overcame) and now you have the 'MAGIC' formula for how they too can overcome their struggle simply by walking through it with you.

This is the message you want to share with people and what you want your potential clients and customers to know about you and how you personally connect - before they even know what you do and how you do it.

Start with your Signature Story of Significance first, and always.

Helpful Hint: This is also the sample story you'd want to include in the 'About Us' section of your website (again, it's not your resume, acknowledgements, awards, achievements or accomplishments).

It's your personal story of overcoming and your biggest opportunity to share your love for what you do (and how you can best serve those that your business product/service was designed to help).

This is where your passion and your pain unite.

It's you, sharing your story.

It's a moment in the spotlight where you highlight where you once were and how you got here.

This is one of my favorite ways to connect with future clients and make things interesting by using highlights of how I've turned my struggles into my success.

It's important to talk about the transition to your transformation by sharing pieces of your past personal and professional life to make your story interesting, unique, and all yours – unlike any others.

This sets the tone for how your potential clients will relate to you and want to work with you.

No one else can tell your story like you.

THE MESSAGING MAGIC THINK TANK

The Messaging MAGIC Story Think Tank helps you with thinking through your story while focusing on your results, testimonials, and raving reviews.

People love to hear the stories behind a business brand and why you're so passionate about what you do– and that's something worth getting help thinking through.

While putting together my message/story (and the process I just shared with you), I weeded out what was needed.

I also pieced together stories from my work that brought me the most results, showed the greatest experience of my clients and prove my passion for what I do (and who I do it for).

When you do this, your process will be much easier (and faster).

It helps when you pull from your own collection of positive personal and client-based, results-driven moments that promote your product or service and easily convey your 'MAGIC' message.

If you're thinking, *"AJ, I don't have as many client stories or testimonies as I would like."*, it's okay.

The Story Think Tank will help you discover ways to create MAGIC in your message starting with you as your best and first testimonial of your work along with how you're setting the trend and helping others.

The following questions are great starting points for stories used during your media interviews, Speakers panels, and round table discussions.

These questions are also ideally asked during a 'Hot Seat' coaching session.

People want to know how you came to do what you do versus you just sharing what you do in your business.

---

1. **Why are you so passionate about what you do in your business?**

2. **How do you stand out as a Leader in your industry/field? What makes you different?**

3. **What's the #1 result people can expect after working with you? Can you share a past client's experience?**

4. **What are you hoping to accomplish in your business?**

5. **What exciting new thing coming up in your business this year?**

Answer the following questions in your own personal journal or notebook:

People love an artful story.

You can also leave out "the dirty details" of your story – if you're not careful, this could cause old feelings rise up and send you into an emotional state of dysfunction.

We don't want that.

As you share, make sure your story is:

1. From the heart
2. A reflection of *who* you are as a business person
3. Not full of the "*how*" you work with your clients (leave out your systems and processes)
4. Clear on *what* your potential future new clients will walk away with (your systems, solutions, outcomes, and results)

Once your people "buy-in" to your story of significance, you will be able to share the details of your step-by-step formula for how you help him/her get the results they desire.

You'll also be able to share more about the experience of working with you.

Your goal in sharing your story is to get potential customers or clients to see their current struggle in your story in a way that leads them to sign-on or subscribe to you as the expert with their solution.

You should share your story in a way that will help your clients visualize achieving their own results.

Also remember to give your listeners a call-to-action (CTA) that tells them what to do next to connect with and potentially work with you.

Flip back a few pages to my story's ending where I encourage listeners and readers (potential clients) to take a certain specific action for their next steps in us doing business together.

You can sprinkle your own personal and professional touch in a way that shows you care (and that your future client's business goals mean more to you than just their money).

When you do this right, it's like you've struck gold!

Before you share your story, I encourage you to preview the questions below and write out or summarize your answers in your journal in 2-3 bullet points for the main things you want to be sure to address in your story/ message.

This will help you with the ease of flow.

One of the best ways to get into your story (on and off camera) is to answer each of the following questions:

1. Who are you?

2. What did you use to do before you went into business for yourself?

3. Why do you currently do what you do in your business?

4. What is your background as it relates to your current business?

5. How long have you been in business?

6. Why are you so passionate about your business?

7. When did you realize how important your business was in your life?

8. What difference has your business made in your life?

9. How did you discover the solution your business currently provides?

10. Who do you think needs to hear you share your story?

11. What do you want your audience members/listeners to get out of your sharing?

12. What is the one thing that you are most proud of experiencing personally as it relates to your business story?

13. What is the one thing that you are the most embarrassed about experiencing personally, as it relates to your business story?

14. Why should your listeners pay attention to you and your business story?

15. Based on your knowledge of your business, how can you help your listeners the most?

16. What is your call-to-action (CTA)? – More on that coming up – This should be a challenge from you to your listener to take action. For example, you may say something like, *"I challenge you to…"* or, *"I encourage you to…"* or, *"I want to invite you to…"*

Once you've completed this assignment, I encourage you to share your audio or video recording with a friend, family member or colleague to see if they "get" what you do, how you do it, who you do it for, and why you do it in your business.

ACTIVITY: Get more BONUS points and extra credit if your share your new super-sexy signature business story on Facebook LIVE, Instagram LIVE, Instagram Stories, and/or Snap Chat (or whatever new social media livestream, broadcast, or audio app is currently out).

I encourage you to share your 'Messaging MAGIC' by putting your message out into the world to see the support and response you get.

Need more encouragement to 'GO LIVE'?

Type in your business (or story topic) and see who – if anyone – in the world is sharing a story similar to yours via livestream video and look at how they're doing it to get inspired to GO LIVE!

Your goal is to help others understand how you can help them with what you shared in your story via your step-by-step system (just like you're currently going through with me!).

[ALIGN]:

[ALIGN]:
USING THE FOUR KEYS

T*he* 4 key components of your story might convince a potential new client that you're just what they need (here's where you'll want to take note in your own personal journal):

Key #1 is your struggle. What have you personally been through? This is the same struggle that got you started in business.

Key #2 is your solution. How did you overcome the struggle? This is preferably your simple, step-by-step solution to the struggle above. You should list out at least five steps you took to get "here".

Key #3 is the sell. How can your journey to where you currently are in your business potentially help a future client? This is where you "sell" your solution and help shift their current mindset regarding who you are and what you do.

Key #4 is your success. Your new potential customer(s) and client(s) need to see (and believe) that you're the expert to help them achieve the same super-sexy success you've reached on your own business journey (using your solution to the struggle above as the strategy for how you'll help them 'get there'). It gives them a reason to believe and buy from you.

The BONUS is your call-to-action (CTA): This is the key component to ending (and why you share) your story; Walk people through the process of how they can connect with you to learn more about next steps to working with you – do you want them to call you, email you, visit your website, schedule a meeting, and/or sign up for your email list to learn more about your business products or services?

In your journal, answer the following:

#1 is your <u>struggle</u> – What have you personally been through that led you to exactly where you are in your business currently?

#2 is your <u>solution</u> – What's your answer to how you overcame your struggle(s), step-by-step?

#3 is the <u>sell</u> – How can you help your potential future customer/client understand how what you've learned and discovered for yourself can potentially help them plus, how can they connect with you to learn more?

#4 is your <u>success</u> – What do they need to know to help them understand why you are the expert to help them achieve the same super-sexy success that you've obtained?

If you've worked up to this point to lay the foundation for what you do and who you do it for, the steps to crafting (and building upon) your speech will help you plug in your findings to this super simple formula.

The following is a working example from my story that I shared with you earlier and still use today using each step of the four keys in my struggle to success story (aka, my 'Story of Significance' and my Super-sexy Signature Speech).

Here's my story:

Key #1: [The Struggle]

It took me fifteen years to graduate college. Ten years ago, I had two corporate jobs downsize, and I became homeless; living in my car, and sleeping on the floors and couches of family and friends. During this transition, I also went through the dissolution of a five-year marriage.

After the divorce trial I left the courtroom and headed down the hallway to get on the elevator to leave the courthouse. I pushed the "Down" button, the elevator opened, and I stepped on – as I saw my ex-husband for the last time.

My phone rang. I answered. It was my cousin calling to tell me my mom had just passed away. She was forty-seven years old.

The drop out, the downsize, the divorce, and death of my mom all turned out to be a business-building blessing in disguise.

How, you ask?

Key #2: [The Solution]

It was during this time that I decided I was tired of being "let go". I no longer wanted anyone to make the decision for me regarding whether I was wanted (or not), when I got paid (or not), how much money I made (or not) or how many hours I worked (or not).
I took some time to sit with myself, God, and all that had occurred in my life - my story.

No more 9-to-5 for me. I was ready to pursue my dream of full-time entrepreneurship. I got this from my mom, my dad, and both of my grandfathers. I'm a third-generation entrepreneur.

I reconnected to my purpose, which is serving the world through sharing my knowledge (teaching/training) women of influence on how to share and sell their stories of significance to make more money in their business and leave a legacy for generations to come.

During the research of my market, I discovered that 70% of women small business owners make less than $25,000 per year, according to the U.S. Women's Chamber of Commerce. I knew it was because they were sharing too much about *what* they do in their business, but now *why* they do it. They didn't have what I now call, 'Messaging MAGIC'.

Key #3: [The Sell]

I spent time networking and connecting with women in business, and I started to understand why they were broke. It was because of what they were saying (more specifically, and more importantly, what they were leaving out – or not saying) about what they did in their business, and *why*. They didn't have 'Messaging MAGIC'.

The key to this crisis is hidden in the power of their personal story.

This simple concept has multiplied the revenue in my business.

It's why I'm sought-out and booked as a paid professional Speaker, Trainer, Author, Story-teller, and the developer of a magical concept for making more money in business.

The 'Messaging MAGIC' method is the solution to business-building, poverty-crushing success.

I'm 'The Messenger'. I coach women entrepreneurs using 'Messaging MAGIC'; a five-part formula that shows you how to tell your business story from your potential client's perspective by sharing how you turned your obstacles into opportunities, why you feel called to share your story (message) in your business and finding proof using your current business success.

It's a repeatable process that proves when you learn how to effectively tell your story you leave a legacy with your words and ultimately make more money in your business. It makes all the difference in how you reach your next client.

With the help of the Founder of a successful global coaching enterprise who shares her own story using 'Messaging MAGIC', you'll learn how to invest time in creating and sharing your story and applying it to your marketing message (which saves you from sharing your MAGIC with the wrong people).

This also makes it easier to connect with a community of your future clients so that when you find them (or vice versa), you're attracted to each other because you're speaking the same magical language.

Key #4: [Success]

This journey led me to obtain a Bachelors of Science in Training and Development, pursue a Master's Degree in Life Coaching, become a Certified Personal Life Coach, and a Master Book/Business Coach, and now a 10x best-selling Author who writes books for women in business – using what I'd learned running my own micro-enterprise (small business).

You can also refer back to my stories of Mel, Renee and of my own course, my story from earlier in this book to see the success from using the 'Messaging MAGIC' story model.

BONUS:

To claim your own success, connect with me more and get help telling your story, and sprinkling a little MAGIC on it join me at www.thebossof.me/mmaudio.

Now It's Your Turn...

The four key areas (and the BONUS) is what you always want to keep in mind when you're answering the question of *"What do you do?!...".*

Remember, the five parts of the 'Messaging MAGIC' formula starts with your story of struggle and ends with your success.

As you might have discovered, when you share your story, you get away from a title, a tagline, and your bio – you start selling you, what you're able to do, who you're able to successfully do it for, and *why* you do what you do.

Now let's discuss how you can target your new message to help bring those you serve best, closer to you.

What you say about what you do in your business will inspire people to work with you and it encourages them to take action towards that goal.

It's the story of you as it relates to how you came to do what you do in your business.

This is your present-day truth.

It's what will impact your future clients the most and help them potentially change their lives for the better.

It's your way to encourage, inspire, engage, support, and challenge the people you serve.

As one of my million-dollar mentors once said, *"People don't buy your services, they buy you!"*

This is all based on their personal experiences with wanting to work with you.

I'm a firm believer that you can only teach what you've been through.

You can only sell you (and what you do) by sharing how your product or service has impacted your own life and how it has changed the lives of others.

Sharing your story helps others (who may want to work with you) see themselves and their current obstacles, issues, challenges, and struggles in what you've been through along with exactly how you can help them.

Your story makes you relatable.

It helps people understand who you are.

It makes potential clients want to know more about you and potentially working with you.

NOTE: Don't worry about sharing exactly *how* can help them (just yet).

Your potential customers/clients need to first understand (and be sold on) the experience of what it's like to get the results they seek (and *how* you can potentially provide them) by working with you.

This is where they'll begin to see how you're the answer to their prayers (remember the quote from the beginning of this book? – no worries, it's at the end too!) just from what you say you can do for them as you share your story.

This is considered the *"what"* in the question, "So, w*hat do you do*?".

So, if you're a technical type who wants to give all of the fill-in-the-blank details of exactly how you do what you do (and take people through the process), this part is for you.

I have no doubt that you are smart and quite possibly great at what you do.

But ask yourself, *"How has sharing all of the details of <u>how</u> I do what I do in my business in an initial conversation with a potential client helped me gain more business in the past?"*

I encourage you to hold off on the *"how"* you do what you do and simply focus on the formula (it's the 'solution' you listed earlier to your future client's needs).

[GUIDE]:

[GUIDE]:
USING THE POWER OF
YOUR STORY

L et's discuss your experience and focus on how what you've been through relates to what you want your future potential customers or clients to know about you and your business.

Be as detailed as possible as you walk through this development and design process.

SET THE SCENE

Here is where you paint a mental picture for your future (potential) customers and/or clients.

I encourage you to use some of what you've shared in the previous section to add to the *'when'* and *'where'* in your personal story about the moment you first decided to go into business for yourself 'when' and 'where' refer to the exact moment or scenario you decided.

Include the following in your answer:

I know these are unusual questions.

- What was the weather like that day?

- What day was it?

- What time of year was it?

- Were you at home, out-and-about, at a meeting, or a friend's house?

- Was your job downsized (like mine)?

- What city were you in?

- Was the economy good or bad?

Your answers to these questions will be useful in your story.

WHO CARES?

C omplete the following sentience: *"I'm sharing my journey with you, (potential customer/client), because…"* and fill in your answer to this, *"What I really want you to get from my story and what I've been through, (potential customer/client), is…"*.

Use this script to help you wrap up your story.

Finish the above two statements and the question below in your own personal journal:

> What would be the main reason you would want to share this with your people?

[INSPIRE]:

[INSPIRE]:
THROUGH ENGAGEMENT

L et's focus on engagement and how to quickly get you to the point of your story.

The goal is brevity (being brief) when you share with people about what you do in your business.

For example, here's what I believe about what people get wrong when you're asked, *"So, what do you do?"*

The following includes my main thoughts, points, ideas, and opinions on the topic along with supporting sub-points:

The Main Point is the point of your story.

My story's main point is: You must share your story and *why* you're so passionate about what you do in your business when you're asked, *"So, what do you do?"*.

The Sub-point supports the main point of your story.

My story's sub-point is: When you go beyond your bio, title or a tagline and share a bit of your personal/professional story along with *why* you do what you do in your business, you will get more people to buy from you, support you, ask to learn more about what you do, and refer others to you. As a result, you'll then be able to confidently convert conversations into clients, cash, checks, and credit cards.

Get it?

Now, it's your turn.

Take a moment to list out your story's main points and sub-points (which also include your through points, ideas, and opinions).

Then, join me in the next section.

In your own personal journal, complete the following:

My Story's Main Point is:

My Story's Sub Point is:

[CONVERT]:

[CONVERT]:
SELL

Remember the 'Signature Story' you wrote out in the 'Marketing' section, where we discussed the four keys to telling a good story?

Now it's time to put those steps to use to sell what you do while telling your story.

This is referred to as '*story-selling*'.

NOTE: This will become your five-step solution to the problem your future listening audience of potential customers or clients are currently dealing with.

It relates to how you overcame your struggle(s) on your journey to success along with how you can help them overcome their current situation step-by-step.

Look back through your notes and review your system.

Each step you lay out is called a *'deliverable'*.

A deliverable is what you are promising to those you speak with who may be ready to do business with you.

During your story-selling you'll give a brief walk-through of how you get your clients from where they are to where they want to be.

This is summarizing *how* you do what you do.

For example, this book, 'Messaging MAGIC' and the deliverables I promise to you are:

Deliverable #1: We develop your struggle-to-success story.

Deliverable #2: We go over your solution strategy.

Deliverable #3: We dive into selling your solution strategy using the power of your story.

Deliverable #4: We design your success strategy for systematic sales.

These deliverables are your secrets that hold the key to helping you build the platform you need to create buyers of your business products and services.

When you tell your story of struggle and solution people will be sold on your success and theirs.
This is where the MAGIC comes into your messaging.

Finding the MAGIC in your message helps more people listen and make better, faster decisions to do business with you.

What are your deliverables? List them in your journal.

WHAT IS IT GOOD FOR?

Now get ready to tell your listening audience of potential purchasers of your products and services who your five-step system is good for and who it will work for.

Think back to who you were when you first began your entrepreneurial journey.

Capture a mental picture of yourself when you needed the information you have to offer right now to help someone else.

Before I discovered 'Messaging MAGIC' concept, I was one of the women business owners who wanted to stop feeling like I was begging people to do business with me.

I needed to get more customers and clients.

I wanted to make more money in my business.

But I first needed to learn how to win my potential customers and clients over to the idea of working with me.

I also wanted to do all of this without feeling stressed out or overwhelmed about marketing my business.

I wanted more people to buy from me, support the sales and events I had going on in my business.

I wanted them to listen to me and learn more about what I did in m business and be able to refer other business to me.

I also wanted them (and their friends, fans, and followers) to return to do business with me again in the future.

I wanted to stop blending in and start standing out in my industry (coaching) in an authentic way.

I now know how to do that and will show you how – using the power of story.

What is your system good for and who will it work for? Write it in your journal.

GOOD RIDDANCE

Now let's tell your potential customers/clients what they'll be able to get rid of once they're sold on your story of struggle, your success, and your solution.

Here's an example,

After you read *Messaging MAGIC*, you'll get rid of:

1. **Taking taglines and titles that come with the frustration and overwhelm from people "not getting it" when you answer the question,** *"So, [insert your name here] what do you do?"*

2. **The question,** *"What does sharing my story or "telling my business" have to do with brining in or making more money in my business?"*

3. **The question,** *"What part of my story do I share?"*

4. **The question,** *"How do I share my story and tie it in with what I do in my business to help bring in new customers or clients?"*

When I was first figuring this 'story' stuff out, I ran into a huge road block.

I didn't know *how* to share my story.

I spent lots of hours (and dollars) weeding through information and trying to figure out an efficient way to handle this 'story problem'.

I spent over three years developing an easier way to help you (and me) make more money by sharing our story/message.

The bad news is, I went through this struggle alone.

The good news is, you don't have to.

I didn't want women entrepreneurs (like you) to struggle with this too.

I made it easy for you to not have to 'recreate the wheel' of story-telling.

Hence, the creation of 'Messaging MAGIC', the book, the masterclass, the course, the workshop, the live events, and so much more!

When you use the tools I've shared with you and the story you've created during our time together, you'll save yourself the loads of time and money I had to invest to develop this system.

You'll also save what could have been months (or years) of trial and error of wasted time and money - because you're getting it right the first time.

What does your system/solution help people get rid of?

Answer the following:

---

1. **What will your system will help them do?**

2. **What will your system will help them get rid of?**

3. **What has your system has done for you and/or at least one of your previous clients successfully?**

In the next section, you'll tell your potential new customers/clients how much your new system costs and why they should get started working with or doing business with you today.

This is what I've just walked you through, using the 'Messaging MAGIC' formula.

This may seem like a lot of work.

It is.

It's also necessary.

With all that we've created together up to this point, you're now well on your way to telling (and selling) your story using your 'super sexy' struggle-to-success signature system.

Keep going.

See you in the next section on how to price your new message.

[PRICE TO PROFIT]:

[PRICE-TO-PROFIT]:
THE MONEY BEHIND THE
MESSAGE

---

*"She is successful because her burden became her blessing. Because
she has a story to tell, it makes it easier for her to sell."*
- Lewis Howes

Pricing your new story/solution/system is one of the most important steps in sharing your MAGIC message with the world.

This is the space where you get to dig deep into how to put a price on your service(s) and/or your product(s) and include it in your story-selling.

Soon, we'll review how you can confidently quote your prices within the process of sharing your new story/message.

Putting a price on your message can also lead to frustration.

However, once you've worked your way through this section you will have discovered how to overcome and avoid one of the biggest setbacks in making more money in your business - being able quote your price with confidence.

You may feel a little uncomfortable, but I encourage you to keep moving forward.

Learn how to set a rate for your products and services as you share your new message in a way that one of my millionaire mentors says, *"Shows the world how much you value what you do"*.

This process puts a number/amount on the work you do using your message and your new step-by-step system of success.

Think of putting a price with your message as a reward you get for showing up to leave your mark on the world.

It's your next step to instantly increasing your impact, influence, and income in your business.

Just know that you'll reach who you're meant to serve through the power of your story – by putting a price on it.

With this pricing process you'll be able to sell your potential customers and clients during your conversation.

Eventually, they'll begin to trust you with the magical sixteen-digit number on their credit card (even if you don't consider yourself to be "a numbers person").

Let's discuss how much you're going to charge them when they start showing up ready to do business with you.

Your price for your products or your service rates show others just how serious (and professionally) you take what you do in your business.

The higher your pricing, the better (and the more value and respect you'll potentially bring to your business brand).

Your money goal may not be to be the highest priced in your industry.

It also shouldn't be to be the lowest priced either.

Choosing from the following options below, which one(s) do you want your potential customers/clients to say?...

1. *"Wow! That's a great price."*
2. *I've heard great things about the value of what you do through your work and that it's worth every penny. Sign me up!"*
3. *"This is exactly what I need. I'm ready to buy!"*
4. *"I can tell you know your stuff and you are the person I need in my life."*
5. *"What's my next step? Where do I sign up?"*

Hopefully you selected all of the above.

Consider this when pricing your products/services using your new message.

Your pricing is what you tell yourself and those who need you and what you do in your business that this is the dollar amount you believe your time, talent, knowledge, gifts, experience, expertise and training in your field is worth.

The lower you price yourself and what you do, the cheaper your brand value will be perceived.

When you price too low your business brand becomes stereotyped as not worth it.

Price up and give yourself a chance to stop blending in and start standing out in your industry.

Give your clients a head-start on seeing what you're worth, experience the results you give them through your business products and services, and allow them to vote with their words and their wallets.

Next, let's discuss how to:
1. Make more money doing what you love while sharing the power of your story
2. Put a price on your products and/or services while sharing *why* you do what you do
3. Set a rate that puts a value on what you do, as you sprinkle your MAGIC message
4. Establish the respect that you and your business brand deserve through story-selling

I hope you're ready to show up and shine with confidence in your rate as I also walk you through my story of how my clients

First, established my rate for me

Then, told me my value (voted with their words)

And, voted with their wallets (and paid me more than I was charging at the time)

A MAGIC MONEY STORY

When I first started out as a professionally paid Speaker, I was invited to share my story and expertise with a small group of about fifteen aspiring business women on a topic pertaining to business-building and making more money in their business.

During the initial phone call when I spoke with the event Hostess and agreed to speak at her event, we never discussed pricing (a fee I would charge to show up and shine while sharing my MAGIC with her audience).

At the event, I spoke to the group for about thirty minutes sharing my story and showing the power of what I do as a Master Coach.

I left that event with a check for one-hundred-and-fifty dollars.

This is when I realized that this client and her audience voted with their words (via a raving review and testimonial during the event).

Then, the Hostess voted with her wallet (by writing me a check for my professional speaking and story-telling services).

She put an actual dollar amount on the value she believed I brought the audience of ladies at her event along with the knowledge I shared with her people.

This helped me put a dollar amount on my fee for a half-hour talk to share my story about what I do to bring value to an audience of women who needed it.

I then nearly doubled that payment amount and started quoting my new hourly rate of two hundred and ninety-seven dollars to speak and share my story at future events.

How cool is that?

This is a perfect example of pricing your 'Messaging MAGIC'.

So, now let's talk about what that looks like for you.

> **When you're invited to speak to a group and be paid to share your new message/story about what you do in your business, who you do it for (and why), what rate will you quote?**

Here's a question and a pricing activity for you:

Write the amount in your journal.

This amount should make you feel happy and maybe even nervously excited to be in a position to charge this amount to your potentially new customers or clients.

It should be enough to make you smile each time you are paid that amount.

Now, whatever amount you have in mind (and have written down), multiply it by two - like I did.

How do you feel about believing in yourself enough to charge twice as much to share your new message?

NOTE: According to some state guidelines, if you're a one-income, small business owner brining in less than $1,300 per month from your business, you're considered to be at a very low-income/poverty level – remember that startling statistic I shared with you at the beginning of this book? So, it's up to you to charge more than enough to overcome this statistic by pricing up.

This all came to light for me recently when I was blessed with the opportunity to dine (lunch, dinner, and behind-the-scenes access) with 'The God-Mother of Transformation' herself, Lisa Nichols, from the movie, 'The Secret' (she's also been seen on The Oprah Winfrey Show, The Steve Harvey Show, and more) – see our picture at www.thebossof.me.

During our time together, we "talked shop" (profits, numbers, vision-casting for my business growth, success, and so much more).

Our connection and conversation was the defining moment I needed for myself and my growing business as I received insight, spiritual downloads, and an overall new perspective on how to triple (yes, triple!) the revenue I was already generating in my business, using 'Messaging MAGIC', telling my story and putting a much bigger price tag on it.

My MAGIC system of struggle, solution, and success was set to sell.

But first, it had to be 'priced to profit'.

ANOTHER MONEY MAGIC STORY

A few years ago, I was a Room Monitor, a Facilitator, a Presenter, and a Consultant for a series of three consecutive events for a large conference.

More than five hundred people attended this annual event.

One hundred or so of them were service professionals who would have been considered my perfect client market at the time.

One year, as the event came to an end I left my business card with the event organizer and encouraged her to contact me whenever I was needed for future events.

A few weeks later, the organizer called me to extend an opportunity for me to teach a small group of those same community leaders for a total of twenty-four hours of my time and I would be paid $5,000.

That was five thousand dollars for only one day of my time!

If you do the math, that was about the $297 per hour rate I had previously set for my professional speaking services.

Pretty cool, huh?

I was priced to profit.

> # QUESTION:
>
> Does your new price for sharing your new story/message match your daily, weekly, monthly, or yearly monetary goals?
>
> If you answered "No", I encourage you to once again double the fee you wrote down previously.

NOTE: When you put a significant value on your product(s) and service(s), your business becomes more open to bringing in more than enough income to meet (and exceed) your needs.

This allows you to have extra to invest in the lives of those you serve.

Remember, in the end, your business product or service is not just about you.

It's also about having the financial resources to assist yourself and others with living your best lives and leaving a legacy for generations to come.

You are in business to provide a product or service that people are willing to pay you for.

Why wouldn't you allow them to do that?

Payment for your business-based products and services is a physical form of a "Thank You" for potentially changing the course of your customer or client's life.

Whether you mentor teens, coach business owners, are a Life Coach, a Travel Agent, an Event Planner or a Video Producer, you are in a position to make change happen through the MAGIC if your message.

I encourage you to confidently quote a price for it.

Take advantage of the opportunity to instantly increase your impact, influence, and income simply by deciding that you, your business products and services are worth it.

Believe that what you have to offer matters, is needed, and is valued.

People are willing to pay you for it.

Will you quote them your new price and let them do so?

Commit to it and stick with it.

Doesn't it feel great to be able to decide what your story is worth?

Something awesome to note here is when you stick with your new price, the right customers and clients are drawn to doing business with you – often because they'll sense and see the confidence you have in your pricing for your products and services.

Your new rate should cause one of the reactions you selected a few pages back when you quote it to your future customers/clients.

It should also stir up the drive and determination within them to afford to work with you because they know the value you have to offer.

BIG MISTAKE

A void the mistake of pricing your products or services like you (or someone you know) might shop, looking for the best deal and the lowest price.

You don't want to be the bargain basement store of pricing in your industry.

I was once told that there's usually something irregular about cheap items.

When you undercharge for your products or services, you often are frustrated afterwards and wishing you would have charged more.

Trust me on that one.

You never know what people are willing to spend until you quote your price and invite them to invest with you.

By doing so, you are increasing your chances of success.

Two of the biggest setbacks in pricing is fear and comparing yourself to others.

This will always hold you back from quoting and sharing your new, higher price.

It's not your business what everyone else is doing.

People are waiting to pay you.

QUESTION:

What's the reason you want to make more income in
your business?

That should be your main focus.

List this in your journal.

Your reason can (and will) help you instantly increase your impact,
influence, and income.

Next, spread the word and share your story, your struggle-to-success
solution system, and your pricing with others.

Watch and receive the positive reactions and energy of new and
potential customers and clients flow to you.
The 'Messaging MAGIC' formula works, when you work it.

THE END

Together, we've traveled through your story to help you map out your magical message, step-by-step – like:

1. How to navigate through and share your story using the MAGIC formula

2. Designing your signature 'struggle-to-success' story/system

3. Creating a system for selling your story of struggle-to-success and your solution successfully, along with how to put a price on it

You also now know what your step-by-step system will get rid of, what is has helped you do, and what it will help your potential customers or clients be able to do (your deliverables).

You've also seen how your story and your professional proficiencies are also significant, plus, how to include them in your story-selling process (along with the *"how"* you do what you do).

You have access to this system for how to stay relevant when you share your message/story using the perfect speech model I've shared with you within the last few pages.

You have your new magical money-making message for your business.

Keep practicing.

Continue working to develop the parts of your story that you want to keep and what "dirty details" you want to leave out.

'Messaging MAGIC' helps you master your message and your story in a way that's just right for you and your business.

It's designed to help you tell and sell your story while leaving a legacy with your words by having the blue print to sharing your marketing message in a way that helps you know what to say and what to leave out.

This step-by-step system shares top tips on what to say when you're selling *you* and it gives you the clues on how to do it.

Whether you're introducing yourself to one person at a networking event or speaking to a few hundred people from a global stage, it's necessary for you to learn how to tell your story and relate it to why you do what you do in your business.

The secrets in this book have revealed to you how:

1. The only way for you to get more people to buy from you, support you, and learn more about what you do (and tell others about you) is through your MAGIC message.

2. The only way to effectively share your message and see the results above is through 'Messaging MAGIC'.

3. Using these secrets will help you help others fall in love with what you do by using the power of your story about *why* you do what you do in your business.

4. You can win customers/clients without feeling stressed out when telling people about your business.

Now, grab your journal notes from all of the work you've done up to this point and get ready to use your story to magnify your message, market your business, and make more money while doing so, using your super-sexy signature story.

Now it's time to rehearse (and soon reveal to the world) your new super-sexy signature speech you've crafted during our time together.

Please Note

Practice DOES NOT make perfect, but it sure does help!

I'm challenging you to share your new speech with a few of your favorite friends, fans, and followers for feedback.
As you share, listen for clarity, confidence, conversational flow (this is when you share your story as naturally as you speak to someone else in an everyday conversation – you don't want to sound stiff, or like you're reading a script or reciting from memory).

Be sure to listen to the heart of your 'this is who I am', and 'this is what I do' message delivery.

Aim to make how you share your speech full of your own natural voice and tweak your speech as needed.

I encourage you to share your story often when you speak of your business.

You now have your new answer for 'what you do' (and *why*).

Here's the 'Messaging MAGIC' formula recap to help you make sure your message:

Step 1: Markets – Tells your potential customers/clients the results you bring that they want or wish for

Step 2: Aligns – Lines up and matches the outcome (you're hoping for) of your speech

Step 3: Guides – Holds their hand on your journey

Step 4: Inspires – Brings people up (lifts their spirits and leaves them there)

Step 5: Converts - Gets people to raise their hands to get what they want or wish for from you

The secrets you've learned during our time together will build on the platform you need to create buyers of your products and services in your business because you are clear on who your system will work for (and who it won't), plus what results your people can expect from working with or doing business with you.

You now know what your step-by-step stem will get rid of, what it has helped you do, and what it will help your potential clients be able to do (also known as your *deliverables*).

My promise to you is if you:
- Follow the formula that's been laid out for you in this easy-to-follow guide
- Commit to memory the secrets that have been shared with you
- Implement and take action on what you have learned (and written out)

You will instantly increase your impact, influence, and income while sprinkling your own MAGIC on your message as you share it all over the world.

Don't be what Business Investor, Mark Cuban of the show, 'Shark Tank', describes as the *'wantrepreneur'*.

I define this as someone who *knows* she's not making the money she deserves and desires in her business but fails to make a move to do something about it.

Not taking immediate action means that you secretly may be okay with the way things are in your business right now and you're guaranteed to be exactly where you are today by this time next year, not making enough money and letting clients and/or customers slip right through your fingers and move on to working with someone else.

Be the business woman who decides that enough is enough and recognize that this is a sign and an answer to your prayers for the opportunity to do and be more in your life and in your business.

When your potential customers or clients hear you speak passionately about *who* you are (your story), *what* you do (featuring the results, benefits, and outcomes), and *why* they want you to help them (your own personal story and professional expertise based on your past experience), they will be impressed and honored to do business with you.

The tips on 'Messaging MAGIC' that you've learned have been proven to capture attention (as you've witnessed if you've heard me speak, introduce myself, and share my own testimony – like I've done in this book! And like you will witness in the BONUS resources over at www.thebossof.me/mmaudio) and captivate the hearts of those who need what only you can provide.

All you have to do is make the decision to move forward with mastering your magical message and let go of your old elevator pitch that you know is not working and has never really served you to help you bring in much business in the past.

Each step of 'Messaging MAGIC' that you've completed so far offers you the insight you need for being the stand out business leader at any networking event or with any small or large crowd of people when you share who you are and what you do.

Take your business back by becoming a Master of your message (and your money) while wooing clients to happily work with you – helping you increase your impact, influence, and income.

So, if you had a super-sexy signature sales story today that was making you money as you were reading this book, what would it be worth to you?

At this point, you have two choices.

Choice #1 is to do nothing.

If you do nothing with what has been shared with you in this book, what will you get?

Nothing.

Or, you can take a leap of faith (like I did) and just test it out to see if 'Messaging MAGIC' will work for you (and if you do it right, it will – I guarantee it).

You have nothing to lose.

Visit www.thebossof.me/mmaudio to get your FREE gift to help you take the next step in adding more MAGIC to your message using the FREE resources that go along with this book!

The goal for this book has been to enlighten you on how to build your confidence in your story/messaging as it relates to helping you sell the products and services your business offers – in a way that confidently converts conversations to clients, cash, checks, and credit cards!

You are now able to quote your prices as you share your message and allow potential clients the space to afford doing business with you.

You are officially better positioned to make more money doing what you love in your business.

When you put a value on what you do, you establish the respect your business brand deserves.

So, show up and shine.

Let your future clients vote with their words and their wallets.

That's how you confidently convert conversations to clients, cash, checks, and credit cards.

ACKNOWLEDGEMENTS

This book is in acknowledgement of…

Kenny and Tamiko Pugh, thank you for inviting me on-board to serve with you as a Lead Trainer on the Fast Coach Training team with the vision to train and certify Personal Life Coaches around the world.

Dr. Michael J. Duckett, thank you for trusting me to connect future internationally recognized Personal Life Coaches to their destiny of, *"Helping people think better"*.

Jane Martin, thank you for being such a fun client to work with and my traveling support back-in-the-day – and for listening to all of my crazy stories about the "behind-the-scenes" of business!

The Douglasville Business-to-Business (B2B) and First Fridays crew, thank you for acknowledging and accepting me, embracing my gift of becoming The Boss Of Me, and for allowing me to practice my story, aka, 'Messaging MAGIC', on you!

Dr. Alfred Watkins of the Bronner Business Institute [BBI], thank you for consistently extending the invitation for me to share my gifts and serve God's people to their next level in the business world alongside you and your team.

Amber Wilburn and The Douglas County Chamber of Commerce's 'Young Professional Connections', you supported my path to leadership and my journey to success in being The Boss of Me. I heart you!

Mr. Lou Robinson, Venetta, Lorraine, and the team of Mercer Bears who sat by my side in life-changing meetings, purchased my books, and shared encouraging words that covered me. Thank you!

Dr. Laurie Lankin, Ruby Byers, and Breezy Stranton, thank you for convincing me to get my degree specializing in Training and Development (since it was, *"something I was already doing professionally in my business anyway"* (your words!).

Professor Patricia Prater, thank you for supporting me in our private office chats, and for sowing into my ministry to serve and support women in business.

Professor Dethra Giles; Thank you for seeding the hustle!

The Station Loft Works team, thank you for providing a peaceful space within a co-working environment for me to write.

Fredia, Tinesha, Juanita, Linda, Regan, Cynthia, Mark, Nicole, LaToya, Chanel, Brandi, and Marilyn, for pre-purchasing your copies of this book (what seemed like years in advance) – and not requesting a refund. Thank you! – If I left anyone out, I owe you 😊

The American Public Gardens Annual Symposium Executives for advancing the completion of this book! Thank you.

Every job that "down sized" or "decided to go another way"; Thank you!

ABOUT THE AUTHOR

Award-winning Entrepreneur, best-selling Author of multiple books, Master Book Coach, Business Coach and Life Coach, Professional Speaker, Trainer, and Story-teller.

Going from homelessness, job downsizings, divorce and death of her mother - on the same day - she is the living definition of her name, which means 'strong and courageous'.

Once she realized poverty is a mindset and self-empowerment is the key to turning obstacles into opportunities in life and business using the power of your story to help build a legacy, she set out on a mission to help change the statistic that 70% of women small business make less than $25,000 per year.

She received over $100,000 in scholarships to complete her degree specializing in training and development from Mercer University, soon-after enlisting in a movement to train and certify life coaches around the world.

AJ Austin taught herself how to share a good story and use it as leverage to instantly increase your impact, influence, and income. She is the best in her field as a world-class Coach, facilitating trainings that teach business leaders how to confidently convert conversations to clients, cash, checks, and credit cards.

Ms. Austin also runs the internationally recognized, multi-million dollar ministry division of a life coach training and certification company, where she leads and facilitates the teachings for those wishing to use their life experience, along with this training to add additional streams of income by becoming a Coach, and learning how to share their story in a self-published book.

She has impacted hundreds of thousands through online and offline symposiums, panels, conferences, workshops, private trainings, coaching, and mentoring.

She's a business owner with hundreds of clients and partners around the world, a best-selling Author of several empowering books, including, *'Messaging MAGIC'* [How to Confidently Convert Conversations to Clients, Cash, Checks, and Credit Cards!] and *Secrets of A Socialprenista* [The Top 8 Mistakes Women Entrepreneurs Make That Leave Them Broke, Stuck, and Struggling In Their Business – and she gives them inspiration for the journey].

Her books and training materials and coaching programs are distributed in Australia, The Cayman Islands, Vietnam, The United Kingdom and all across North America.

AJ Austin, then founded, 'The Boss Of Me', an encouraging, empowering, and educational online platform that helps women become Authors and leave a legacy for generations to come, and has launched hundreds of trainings in a virtual community to help aspiring and established Authors stand in authority and be recognized for what they've been through and successfully came out of that can now help others succeed.

From homeless to highly-respected, today, AJ is the recipient of the 'Saving Our Families and Children' Economic Empowerment Award, and the Mercer University Training and Development 'Outstanding Accomplishment' award.

She has served and shared the stage with Speaker Greats like Lisa Nichols, Suzanne Evans, Marie Forleo, Lisa Sasevich, Brandy Harvey, and has been a guest panelist for the United States Small Business Administration.

Have AJ speak, train, and/or facilitate at your next panel, workshop, conference, summit or symposium!

Her goal is to encourage, empower, and educate millions of women around the world. She regularly travels, speaks and trains in an effort to fulfill this mission.

Her calendar fills several months in advance ☺.

Email aj@thebossof.me or call The Boss Of Me offices at (770)744-4475 today.

Friend, Fan, and Follow her on Facebook and Instagram
@messagingmagic
where she does LIVE trainings

WHAT'S NEXT?...

This book has been a brief break down of a more advanced, step-by-step online training called, 'Messaging MAGIC'.

I love sharing gifts!

As my gift to you, I invite you to visit www.thebossof.me/mmaudio to get your FREE gift to help you take the next step in adding more MAGIC to your message, using the FREE audio that goes along with this book!

Ready to put your MAGIC message in a book? Call AJ's office at (770)744-4475 today.

Click here to leave a book review for this book on Amazon.

If you've enjoyed our time together in this book, you may also enjoy seeing me teach, 'Messaging MAGIC' and the more intensive and advanced story-selling techniques LIVE!

I would love to have you as my special guest.

To save your seat on one at/on one of my future events, visit www.thebossof.me/mmaudio.

I'm looking forward to seeing you there.

Remember…

"There is someone somewhere waiting on you to share your story so they can share theirs. When you impact one life, you impact generations. It's when you let your light shine, you give others permission to do the same. I wish you a worldwide influence where you share your story and people hang on to your every word and lives and destinies are changed."

P.s. – Tell your story. People are waiting.